Cambridge Elements ≡

Elements in New Religious Movements
edited by
James R. Lewis
Wuhan University
Rebecca Moore
San Diego State University

THE SOUND CURRENT TRADITION

A Historical Overview

David Christopher Lane
Mt. San Antonio College

CAMBRIDGE
UNIVERSITY PRESS

CAMBRIDGE
UNIVERSITY PRESS

University Printing House, Cambridge CB2 8BS, United Kingdom

One Liberty Plaza, 20th Floor, New York, NY 10006, USA

477 Williamstown Road, Port Melbourne, VIC 3207, Australia

314–321, 3rd Floor, Plot 3, Splendor Forum, Jasola District Centre,
New Delhi – 110025, India

103 Penang Road, #05–06/07, Visioncrest Commercial, Singapore 238467

Cambridge University Press is part of the University of Cambridge.

It furthers the University's mission by disseminating knowledge in the pursuit of
education, learning, and research at the highest international levels of excellence.

www.cambridge.org
Information on this title: www.cambridge.org/9781009048583
DOI: 10.1017/9781009047821

© David Christopher Lane 2022

First published 2022

A catalogue record for this publication is available from the British Library.

ISBN 978-1-009-04858-3 Paperback
ISSN 2635-232X (online)
ISSN 2635-2311 (print)

The Sound Current Tradition

A Historical Overview

Elements in New Religious Movements

DOI: 10.1017/9781009047821
First published online: June 2022

David Christopher Lane
Mt. San Antonio College
Author for correspondence: David Christopher Lane, dlane@mtsac.edu

Abstract: The practice of listening to subtle, inner sounds during meditation to concentrate and elevate the mind has a long history in various religions around the world, including Islam, Christianity, Hinduism, Buddhism, Jainism, and Sikhism. Today there are a number of new religious movements that have made listening to the inner sound current a cornerstone of their teachings. These groups include the Radhasoamis (and their various branches), the Divine Light Mission, Eckankar, the Movement of Spiritual Inner Awareness (MSIA), MasterPath, the Sawan-Kirpal Mission, Quan Yin/Ching Hai, Manavta Mandir, the ISHA Foundation, and a number of others. In this study we provide a historical and comprehensive overview of these movements and how they have incorporated listening to the inner sound as part of their spiritual discipline. We are particularly interested in the distinctive and nuanced ways that each group teaches how to listen to the inner sound current and how they interpret it in their own unique theologies.

Keywords: Shabd Yoga, Radhasoami, Eckankar, Sant Mat, Nada Yoga

ISBNs: 9781009048583 (PB), 9781009047821 (OC)
ISSNs: 2635-232X (online), 2635-2311 (print)

Contents

Introduction

The practice of listening to subtle, inner sounds during meditation to concentrate and elevate the mind has a long history in various religions around the world, including Islam, Christianity, Hinduism, Buddhism, Jainism, Sikhism, and other spiritual movements (K. Singh 1973; Khan 1996; Beck 2009).

Even Western-based religious traditions, particularly certain gnostic schools, have mentioned listening to a divine melody that lifts the soul to higher regions. The Nag Hammadi library discovered in 1945 in Upper Egypt, for example, contains the only existing copy of an early manuscript that gives high praise to a spiritual sound. The book *The Gnostic Mystery: A Connection between Ancient and Modern Mysticism* (Diem 1992) features a number of passages that highlight the importance of this sacred melody.

> In the Trimorphic Protennoia it is described in the following way: I am [the Word] who dwells [in the] ineffable [Silence]. I dwell in undefiled [Light] and a Thought [revealed itself] perceptibly through [the great] Sound ... And it [the Sound] exists from the beginning in the foundations of the All.
>
> (Diem 1992: 45)

Later Christian mystics reported hearing a divine melody when enraptured in prayer, as Richard Rolle of the fourteenth century confessed in his mystical treatise *Fire of Love*.

> But when half a year, three months and some weeks had passed by – during which that warmth of surpassing sweetness continued with me – there was borne in on my perception a heavenly spiritual sound, which pertains to the song of everlasting praise and the sweetness of the invisible melody. Invisible I call it because it can be neither known nor heard except by him to whom it is vouchsafed; and he must first be purified and separated from the world. For while I was sitting in the same chapel, and chanting psalms at night before supper, as I could, I heard as it were the tinkling music of stringed instruments, or rather of singers, over my head. (Rolle 1996: 38)

Other Christian mystics have also alluded to a divine sound or melody. Jakob Böhme (1575–1624), in his text *Aurora* (Böhme 1914), speaks of hearing a plethora of musical instruments as if they were played by a divine orchestra and reached out toward eternity.

D. Scott Rogo (1950–1990), who wrote two books on "paranormal music experiences," makes the argument that hearing mystical sounds is a transcultural phenomenon and not merely relegated to those of a religious bent. To back up this assertion, Rogo provides five categories in which individuals report hearing inner melodies, four of which have a bearing here:

1. Persons who hear sounds in a "normal state"
2. Those undergoing a near-death experience (NDE) who hear music and, on occasion, those who attend to them
3. People who have out-of-body experiences (OBEs) or who practice "astral travel"
4. Mystics who report hearing an inner music (Rogo 1970, 1972)

In India the sound current practice has a long history and appears to date back to before the Vedic period.

Mircea Eliade, in *Yoga: Immortality and Freedom* (1970: 390–91), provides suggestive notes on "mystical sounds" and quotes Brhadaranyaka Upanishad and several other Buddhist and Hindu scriptures of antiquity that describe the internal hearing of a bell sound. He also refers to the *Dabestan-e Mazaheb* wherein the author "speaks of meditation on absolute sound."

Although each religion gives a different description of the practice and each has varying interpretations of what listening to the inner sound ultimately means, in Indian religious systems two terms have become predominant: *nad/ nada yoga* and *shabd yoga*. Both terms are more or less interchangeable, though *nad/nada yoga* as a descriptive marker appears more frequently before the nineteenth and twentieth centuries. For example, almost all Radhasoami-related movements use the word *shabd* (Juergensmeyer 1991) and seldom use the word *nad*. As for the etymology of the terms, *shabd* is a Sanskrit term meaning "sound-speech," often used in different contexts to mean eternal and undivided. *Nad* is also a Sanskrit word meaning sound, usually in terms of something sacred or transcendent.

Early figurines discovered in Mohenjo-daro and Harappa in the Indus Valley, which date back to before the Vedas, indicate that some form of yoga was practiced. Yan Y. Dhyansky has given an elaborate argument in his article "The Indus Valley Origin of a Yoga Practice" (1987) that the practice of withdrawing one's consciousness from the body has a long precedence and can be dated to before the Vedas were finalized. "The system of Yoga which originated in the Indus Valley has existed for more than five thousand years and is now moving from being an Indian tradition to becoming the common property of all humanity" (89–108).

In the book *Listening to the Inner Sound Current: The Perennial Practice of Shabd Yoga* (Lane 2018) Diem-Lane and Lane pointed to the ubiquity of sound current practices found throughout the world, arguing that it is reasonable to assume that the interior exploration of one's own consciousness by hearing subtle sounds and contemplating inner light is not merely a cultural artifact restricted to certain geographical regions, but is rather a biological inherency, part of what is neurologically possible among Homo sapiens, which can be potentially accessed by anyone, anywhere and anytime. In short, shabd or nad yoga elicits a structural pathway within one's own neuroanatomies. Yet it is nevertheless evident that the evolution of this practice has cultural and historical variants. Indian spiritual systems, in particular, have defined and refined the technique and have given the most exhaustive treatment of the subject in the world.

Since listening to the inner sound to elevate one's consciousness is a neural possibility within human beings and it most likely has a naturalistic origination, the question we wish to explore in the following sections is how the practice manifested over time in differing geographical regions. What we discovered in researching this from a historical and sociological perspective is that the modus operandi of concentrating on inner sounds seems intertwined with the theology of the local region. In other words, Christianity's understanding of shabd yoga – a term we use loosely to mean simply any form of meditation that listens to the inner sound for concentration – is invariably explained in light of the Bible, whereas Sikhism's understanding is explained in light of the Sri Guru Granth Sahib. The universal aspect of sound meditation, in other words, is relativized by the historical time and context in which it is practiced.

Today there are a number of new religious movements that have made listening to the inner sound current a cornerstone of their teachings. These groups include the Radhasoamis (and their various branches), the Divine Light Mission, Eckankar, the Movement of Spiritual Inner Awareness (MSIA), MasterPath, the Sawan-Kirpal Mission, Quan Yin/Ching Hai, the Self-Realization Fellowship, Manavta Mandir, the Healthy, Happy, and Holy Organization (3HO), ISHA, and even Theosophy, among others. In this study we provide a historical and comprehensive overview of these movements and how they have incorporated listening to the inner sound as part of their spiritual discipline. We are particularly interested in the distinctive and nuanced ways that each group teaches how to listen to the inner sound current and how they interpret it in their own unique theologies.

However, before we commence detailing the popularity of shabd yoga across a number of new religious movements, it is important to properly understand the historical roots of the practice, particularly as it was developed in India and Persia. Genealogically speaking, almost every new religious movement across the globe that emphasizes listening to the sound current as part of its medita-tional discipline has roots in the Sufi, Sant, and Radhasoami traditions of North India. Why this is so is of special interest since it underlines how religious ideas can spread like memes (Dawkins 1976; Blackmore 2000) across cultural bar-riers and in the process adapt to new geographical locations and audiences.

For example, Eckankar's founder, Paul Twitchell, who started his group in San Diego, California, was a former initiate of Kirpal Singh, whose center of operation, Ruhani Satsang, was in Delhi, India (Lane 1983). Although there are definite similarities between these two groups, Twitchell modified shabd yoga teachings so as to appeal to a more Westernized clientele (Lane 2020a).

It is important to document how a core idea such as listening to the inner sound becomes theologically refashioned when it is subsumed by a new religious movement that wishes to genealogically *dissociate* itself from its predecessors. The reasons for this can be manifold, but it is primarily because the emphasis is on becoming established as a separate entity. The newly emerging religion and its founder disconnect instead of integrate the past from which they arose. This is mostly because there is a tension or fear that if such a past connection is made, the group will attract fewer followers (Lane 1983; K. P. Johnson 1998). Although the essential principle of shabd yoga – hearing inner, subtle sounds to concentrate the mind – may not dramatically change, how one views its purpose and efficacy is open to a variety of fluctuations related to time and place.

In the following section details about the relevant neurobiological basis underlying such a discipline is also explored since it clearly indicates the transcultural nature of the practice. We then focus on how the confluence of Sufism, Sant Mat, yoga, Tantrism, and later Sikhism led to a modern-day articulation of shabd yoga and the efficacy of listening to the inner sound current as an elemental spiritual technique. The goal here is to present a clear and comprehensive historical guidebook to groups that share a genealogical connection/association and a specific yogic technique. In the conclusion we want to explore how shabd yoga-related ideas may take on still newer forms and ways of expression in the future, especially in light of how technologies such as virtual and augmented reality are being employed.

The Neurobiological Basis of Shabd Yoga

The human brain is the most sophisticated operating system known to exist. It has roughly 86 billion neurons and trillions of synaptic connections via a vast labyrinth of axons, dendrites, and other subtle clefts. Although it weighs only three or so pounds, within its enfolded compound resides the most remarkable feature in the known universe – consciousness (Churchland 1986; Doran 2019).

Consciousness is the supreme mystery that enlivens all that we know about the world around us. While most of the time our awareness is projected outwardly in order to help us better survive and adapt in this evolutionary experiment writ large, there are those mystical pioneers who have turned inward to discover where this very consciousness arises from and explore what possibilities it portends (S. Harris 2014). Humans have developed a variety of tools to alter their awareness and make it possible to venture into hitherto uncharted territories of the mind, including the practice of concentrating on subtle musical-like tones. It is intriguing to speculate about how listening to inner sounds originated among early humankind, long before it became codified as a practice. Several hypotheses offer tantalizing suggestions, including early NDEs, sleep paralysis, extended periods of sensory deprivation, chemical alteration, and more. In NDEs, for instance, a significant number of patients reported hearing a beautiful melody (Sriramamurti, Prashant & Mohan 2013).

> I heard what seemed like millions of little golden bells ringing, tinkling; they rang and rang. Many times since, I've heard those bells in the middle of the night. Next I heard humming.
>   Music surrounded me. It came from all directions. Its harmonic beauty unlike earthly vocal or instrumental sounds was totally undistorted.
>
> (Spencer 2011: 38)

Sleep paralysis is often accompanied by a severe feeling of immobility, a numbness where one feels as if frozen. According to a 2011 meta-analysis, "Lifetime Prevalence Rates of Sleep Paralysis: A Systematic Review," "In conclusion, we have reviewed the available literature on lifetime episodes of SP and have found it to be a fairly common experience. Although occurring in less than 8.0% of the general population, it is much more frequent in students and psychiatric patients, and the difference between these latter two groups is surprisingly small" (Sharpless & Barber 2011: 313).

While at first glance one may wonder what sleep paralysis has to do with meditation or yoga, a close analysis shows that it may well have been a triggering point among early humans for a deeper psychic exploration. This is precisely because sleep paralysis is often accompanied by extremely vivid visions that are usually taken as real and not as mere dreamy hallucinations. In some sense, every night we sleep we will undergo varying degrees of "sleep paralysis" since it serves as a biochemical way to inhibit our bodily movements while dreaming. As Patricia Brooks and John Peever explain in their study of sleep paralysis,

> Understanding the mechanisms mediating REM sleep paralysis is clinically important because they could explain the nature of REM sleep disorders such as RBD, sleep paralysis and cataplexy/narcolepsy. RBD results from loss of typical REM atonia, which allows pathological motor activation and dream enactment, which often lead to serious injuries. Conversely, sleep paralysis

and cataplexy result when REM atonia intrudes into wakefulness thus pre-
venting normal behavior and movement. Determining the mechanistic nature
of REM sleep paralysis will improve our understanding and treatment of such
disorders. (Brooks & Peever, 2012: 9785–95)

There is an intriguing parallel here to shabd yoga meditation since one of the
very first signs that the technique is working is a growing numbness and blissful
sensation in the lower extremities of the body. This feeling of immobility
eventually takes over the body and the meditator begins to have vivid inner
experiences. Jagat Singh (1884–1951), the third guru proper in the Beas lineage,
has argued that the feeling of paralysis in the body during shabd yoga meditation
is an indication of inner progress. As he explained in a series of letters to his
disciples:

> The numbness of the lower limbs and a feeling of lightness throughout the
> body are signs of concentration.
> The numbness of the body is the natural result of concentration and
> drawing up of consciousness, and you should count yourself fortunate in
> achieving such satisfactory progress within a very short time. The upward
> pull also is a mark of quick concentration and when it is complete you will see
> the light within and the Sound also will become clearer and finer.
> The gradually increasing numbness of the body is the acid test and a proof
> of the withdrawal of the consciousness, and so far it was very satisfactory.
> (S. B. J. Singh 1959: 169, 181)

Shabd yogis in general, however, have not tried to correlate their inner
journeys with a deeper neurobiological understanding since their practice
has been intertwined for centuries with a gnostic-like theology where the
body and the spirit are viewed as distinct entities (Robinson 1979; Diem-
Lane 2015).

However, if shabd yoga meditation is indeed a neurobiological process, then
there should be telltale signs of such that can be quantified by accurately
measuring the levels of neurotransmitters such as gamma-aminobutyric acid
and glycine in the brain while one is feeling the sensation of conscious paralysis
while meditating. Indeed, one wonders if there are not chemical ways of
inducing the same effect in non-meditators and seeing whether they report
similar experiences as their shabd yoga counterparts.

One hypothesis is that shabd yoga practitioners who experience the onslaught
of numbness in their extremities – which shouldn't be confused with parasthesia,
the sensation that one feels when one's foot goes to "sleep" – during deep
meditation are experiencing a biochemical process that is similar to what happens
when we are asleep and certain neurochemicals manifest to inhibit bodily movements. In other words, shabd yoga induces a conscious sleep paralysis of sorts.

If this is correct, we should be able to ascertain whether gamma-aminobutyric acid and glycine levels are operative (Diem-Lane & Lane 2018).

The brain is a simulator par excellence and when it is deprived of incoming stimuli, it tends to generate a panoply of fantastic narratives, whether in sleep when we dream or whenever certain psychoactive chemicals (organic or artificial) are ingested. Under these conditions the senses become aware of hitherto unknown or unexplored properties. The history of mysticism – East and West – is chock-full of superluminal reports where one experiences inner light, sensations of leaving the body, and hearing enchanting music. These remarkable accounts are generally viewed as indicative of higher spiritual attainment and thus looked upon with favor if they reinforce or legitimize the current thinking of the community (Lane 2019a).

However, today, given our more hyperscientific age, NDEs, OBEs, and religious visions are generally regarded as purely neurological in origin and thus not viewed as paranormal. This is particularly the case with hearing inner sounds that are often explained away as tinnitus, which the Mayo Clinic defines as "The perception of noise or ringing in the ears. A common problem, tinnitus affects about 15 to 20 percent of people. Tinnitus isn't a condition itself – it's a symptom of an underlying condition, such as age-related hearing loss, ear injury or a circulatory system disorder" (Mayo Clinic 2022).

Nad and shabd yoga adherents balk at the suggestion that what they are hearing is merely tinnitus misdiagnosed. They argue that there is a significant difference between the two because shabd elevates while tinnitus irritates. The conflation of tinnitus with the inner sound current is a complicated one and needs further research since even shabd yoga literature describes sounds that have no mystical import. For example, Sawan Singh, the second guru proper in the Radha Soami Satsang Beas lineage, in giving advice to an American disciple categorically states in *Spiritual Gems* that "eight of the [sounds] are local, but the Bell and Conch are connected with higher regions" (S. Singh 1965: 127). By using the term "local" Sawan Singh may be referring to something akin to tinnitus. In any case sound, like light, is not singular but a spectrum of different frequencies and this important distinction must be considered before reducing all internal sounds to the rushing of blood in the head. However, even tinnitus is not yet fully understood by science and it may well be that there is a wider spectrum to how and why certain sounds generate a feeling of bliss and upliftment and others do not. The tinnitus label is most likely too general and a more comprehensive and precise terminology needs to be developed. Arguably, a detailed understanding of neuroanatomy in the future may eliminate our present confusion surrounding what these inner sounds may portend.

Nevertheless, one thing is certain: the meditational practice of nad and shabd yoga is given high praise in several Hindu and Sikh scriptures and it has continually grown more popular over the past two centuries both in India and around the globe.

The History of Nad and Shabd Yoga

In the early commentaries made upon the Vedas known as the Upanishads, much is made of a primeval sound known as Aum/Om that is equated with Brahman/God. One of the earliest such texts that elaborates on the sacred sound is the Chandogya Upanishad, which scholars believe was composed nine to six centuries before the advent of Christianity. The Sanskrit text begins with प्रथमोऽध्यायः ॥ओमित्येतदक्षरमुद्गीथमुपासीत । ओमिति ह्युद्गायति तस्योपव्याख्यानम् which Swami Lokeswarananda (2017: verse 1.1.1.) translates as "Om is the closest word to Brahman. Recite this Om as if you are worshipping Brahman. How you recite this Om is being explained."

A number of other Upanishads elaborate on the power and efficacy of Om, but the one text that elaborates in detail about listening to the inner sound as a foundational spiritual practice is the Nadabindu Upanishad. Scholars are still debating about when it was composed, with dates ranging as far back as the fourth century BCE to the first century CE (Paul 2006). This core text has had a major influence on other yogic manuals, particularly about how to listen to the inner sound and which sounds in hierarchical order one should attend to. A key excerpt from the Nadabindu Upanishad explains the yoga of sound in its essence:

> The yogin being in the siddhāsana (posture) and practising the vaishnavīmudrā, should always hear the internal sound through the right ear. In the beginning of his practice, he hears many loud sounds. They gradually increase in pitch and are heard more and more subtly. At first, the sounds are like those proceeding from – the ocean, clouds, kettle-drum, and cataracts: in the middle (stage) those proceeding from mardala (a musical instrument), bell, and horn. At the last stage, those proceeding from tinkling bells, flute, vīnā (a musical instrument), and bees. Thus he hears many such sounds more and more subtle. When he comes to that stage when the sound of the great kettle-drum is being heard, he should try to distinguish only sounds more and more subtle. (Aiyar 1914: 257)

The literary structure of the Nadabindu Upanishad has become a template for other, later iterations of nad yoga, which almost invariably follow the guidelines laid out two millennia ago. First the practitioner is advised to "always hear the internal sound through the right ear" (Aiyar 1914: 257). Later shabd yoga groups in the Sant and Radhasoami traditions will make this a cardinal feature in their initiation instructions. The reason for this emphasis on the right ear is open to speculation, with many theories abounding. These range from (1) simple sanitation, as the left hand was often used when answering the call of nature in premodern societies, sans toilet paper (Davisson 2020); (2) the predominance of right-handedness in the human population (90 percent versus 10 percent of left-handed orientation); (3) the symbolic/mythological elevation of the right hand; (4) and, arguably, the prescientific intuition that the right ear receives and retrieves sounds better than the left ear. As the Acoustical Society of America reported in 2007, "Listening requires sensitive hearing and the ability to process information into cohesive meaning. Add everyday background noise and constant interruptions, and the ability to comprehend what is heard becomes that much more difficult. Audiology researchers have found that in such demanding environments, both children and adults depend more on their right ear for processing and retaining what they hear" (Acoustical Society of America 2017).

Yogis in the nad and shabd yoga traditions have tended to provide a dramatic and mythological explanation behind why the right ear is preferred to the left ear since the former is of the positive power (Sat Purush) and the latter is part and parcel of the negative power (Kal). As Sawan Singh explains in a letter to one of his American disciples, "In case the strength of the Shabd in the left ear persists, you should relax your concentration and bring your mind out in order to subdue the left ear Shabd, which is to be eschewed as being the sound of the Negative Power, while we have to follow that of the Positive Power which is either from the right side or in the middle" (S. Singh 1965: 56). Yet even this bipolarity is often minimized since nad and shabd yogis argue that the inner sound current eventually comes from the center of the forehead and above.

A number of Upanishads elucidate on Om, shabd, and how the primordial sound is generative of the creation. For example, the Mandukya Upanishad, though compiled several centuries later than the Nadabindu Upanishad, elaborates on the significance of Om in just twelve verses. Some commentators have cautioned that Om and the inner sound current may have distinct meanings, even if both speak of a "soundless sound" (Krishnananda 1997).

While these Upanishads serve as the seeding ground for nad and shabd yoga, later medieval texts offer more technical and specific guidelines for hearing subtle inner sounds during meditation. The *Haṭha Yoga Pradīpikā* elaborates on the practice and what the aspirant will achieve if they attain the highest degree of perfection in the discipline. In just nine verses the text focuses on how the neophyte should close both ears with their fingers and attempt to move from coarser sounds to more subtle ones. The goal is to become so absorbed in the inner nad that all outer noises are left behind. What is most intriguing is how the various melodies are arranged. As Pancham Sinh's translation explains, "In the first stage, the sounds are surging, thundering like the beating of kettle drums and jingling ones. In the intermediate stage, they are like those produced by conch, Mridanga, bells, etc. In the last stage, the sounds resemble those from tinklets, flute, Vînâ, bee, &c" (Sinh 1914: 189).

The ultimate goal of listening to the sound current was to achieve moksha or liberation. Because of its very simple technique (close the ears and listen attentively), this yoga became widely known and adopted by various religious sects in Hinduism, Buddhism, Jainism, Sufism, and Sikhism.

The writings attributed to Goraknath and Nathism repeatedly mention shabd and its efficacy since "the word (shabda) is the Guru and attention (surat or surta) is the disciple" (Gorakhbodh 2007: 1). In a similar vein, the following lines point to the efficacy of the sound current. "In the realisation of the word (Shabda parchai) the mind remains in equipoise" (Gorakhbodh 2007: 1). And "The wordless (nih-shabda) is the key and the word (shabda) is the lock; the unconscious one (achet) is old; the conscious one is young; mind in self-transcendence (unman) is ever aware (chetan)" (Gorakhbodh 2007: 1).

The *Gheranda Samhita* of the seventeenth century is a detailed yoga manual and has had a distinctive influence on other yogic-related movements, including Advait Mat and Prem Rawat's Divine Light Mission. It too goes into detail about which sounds one should hear while meditating.

> At past midnight, in a place where there are no sounds of any animals, etc. to be heard, let the Yogi practice Puraka and Kumbhaka, closing the ears by the hands.
>
> He will hear then various internal sounds in his right ear. The first sound will be like that of crickets, then that of a beetle, then that of bells, then those of gongs of bell-metal, trumpets, kettle drums, mridanga, military drums, and dundubhi, etc.
>
> The various sounds are cognized by daily practice of this Kumbhaka. Last of all is heard the Anahata sound rising from the heart; of this sound there is resonance, in that resonance there is a Light. In that Light the mind should be immersed. When the mind is absorbed, then it reaches the Highest seat of Vishnu (parama-pada). By success in this Bhramari Kumbhaka one gets success in Samadhi. (Vasu 1979: 49)

The Sufi Emphasis on the Sound Current

Listening to the sound current, given its biological roots, also became popular-ized in Sufi-oriented Islam as an efficacious spiritual practice. Hazrat Inayat Khan (1882–1927), writing in the early twentieth century, published an entire treatise on the subject entitled *The Mysticism of Sound and Music*. In the chapter on "Abstract Sound" Khan provides a more universal explanation of the sound current.

> Abstract sound is called Saut-i Sarmad by the Sufis; all space is filled with it. The vibrations of this sound are too fine to be either audible or visible to the material ears or eyes, since it is even difficult for the eyes to see the form and color of the ethereal vibrations on the external plane. It was the Saut-i Sarmad, the sound of the abstract plane, which Muhammad heard in the cave of Ghar-i Hira when he became lost in his divine ideal. The Quran refers to this sound in the words, "Be! and all became." Moses heard this very sound on Mount Sinai, when in communion with God; and the same word was audible to Christ when absorbed in his Heavenly Father in the wilderness. Shiva heard the same Anahad Nada during his Samadhi in the cave of the Himalayas. The flute of Krishna is symbolic of the same sound. This sound is the source of all revelation to the Masters, to whom it is revealed from within; it is because of this that they know and teach one and the same truth.
>
> (Khan 2019: 1–5)

The Chishtīyah order of the Sufis, which has a long history tracing back to Ibrahim ibn Adham of the eighth century, came to India in the twelfth century due to the pioneering work and teachings of Khwājah Muʿīn-ad-Dīn Chishtī (Ernst & Lawrence 2002). The mystics in this tradition focused on trying to achieve unity with God through a series of meditational practices, which included repeating divine names and listening to sacred tones. Famous mystics in this lineage include Baba Sheikh Farid, Amir Khusrau, Salim Chishti, and Inayat Khan. Baba Sheikh Farid would have an outsized influence beyond Sufi-oriented Islam when Guru Nanak, the founder of Sikhism, praised and preserved parts of Farid's poetry. Later, Guru Arjan, the fifth Sikh spiritual leader, incorporated more than 120 of Baba Sheikh Farid's poems in their holy book, Adi Granth, which was later expanded by Guru Gobind Singh into what is now famously known as the Sri Guru Granth Sahib.

In the seventeenth century Sufi mystics Sarmad, Mian Mir, and Mullah Shah praised listening to the inner sound as one of the supreme practices to achieve God-union. In fact, Mullah Shah (Field 2020) described the technique as *sultan-ul-azkar* (king of spiritual practices). One of the more interesting works on this subject comes from the pen of Dara Shikoh, the eldest son of Shah Jahan, the great Mogul emperor who built the wondrous Taj Mahal in Agra, India. After securing initiation from his spiritual guide, Mullah Shah Badakhsi, in Kashmir, Dara Shikoh wrote a short but revealing text in Persian entitled *Risāla-yi Haqq Numāon* (*The Compass of Truth*). Here he openly revealed what had usually been a closely guarded secret among Sufi masters: how to properly use breathing exercises, holy repetition, focused awareness, and listening to the sound current in order to free the petty mind from unnecessary distractions and experience a majestic unity with the Divine (Shikoh 2020).

Dara Shikoh was by all accounts a remarkable scholar, even if he lacked the military prowess necessary to succeed his father, Shah Jahan, as the Mogul emperor. He was fluent in several languages and had a keen interest in spirituality across traditions, foregoing the strident parochialism and narrow-mindedness of more literalist followers of Islam. Historically, the tragedy that still haunts India to this day is that Dara Shikoh was never able to succeed his father as heir apparent. Dara Shikoh's younger brother Aurangzeb ordered his beheading so that Aurangzeb could succeed to the throne, which he did in 1658, declaring his older brother an apostate. Nevertheless, Dara Shikoh has had an outsized influence because of his remarkable writings and for the tolerance he showed to religious expressions differing from his own (Chandra 2019).

What is most remarkable about *The Compass of Truth* is how open and transparent Dara Shikoh was in providing the modus operandi of an erstwhile secret Sufi meditational practice. His elucidation of how to listen to the inner sound and why it is more efficacious than other techniques can be best summarized by one very telling and observant line, which Scott Kugle translates thusly: "There is no practice better than that of hearing this sound. This is because every other practice depends upon the will of the practitioner; if for a moment [one] stops it, the practice ceases. But not so this practice! It does not depend upon the will of the practitioner. It is present and available without ceasing and without interruption at all times" (Kugle & Ernst 2012: 149).

As Dara Shikoh elaborates about the sound current practice,

> O friend! When thou sittest to practice this retention of breath, it is necessary that thou shouldst fix thy attention on thy heart, because in this practice, sounds will be heard coming from within thee. With regard to these sounds Mullah Rum, of the blessed memory, has thus written –
>
> On his lips there is a lock, but his heart is full of secrets. His lips are silent, but his heart is full of sounds.
>
> This sound is sometimes like the sound of a boiling big cauldron, and sometimes like the buzzing heard in the nest of bees and wasps. It is this internal sound that one of the ancient authors has thus alluded: –
>
> "Behold His words, they seem like the sounds of ants when He utters His speech in our ears. The whole universe is illumined with the sunshine of His presence. . . ."
>
> O friend! Do not imagine that this sound is within thee (and therefore a hallucination of thy senses). The whole universe, inside and outside, is full of this sound (it is the great Voice of the Silence).

The practice of hearing the Voice of the Silence is called in the path of the Faqirs, the Sultan-ul-askar or the king of all practices. . . . The third kind is the sound which is boundless and infinite, and which is self-existent from eternity and not caused by anything. This sound has one unchanging pitch and tone, neither increases nor decreases, and in which no modification can ever find its way and which is without cause. (Shikoh 2020: 16–20)

The Sant and Sikh Practice of Shabd and Nam

It is of historical interest to ponder how various religious traditions intersected – from the yogis to the Naths to the Sufis to the Sants to the Sikhs – and how they each in their own distinctive way emphasized listening to the inner sound.

While it is apparent that the Sufi practice of *sultan-ul-azkar* dates back centuries, with some Muslims claiming that the founder of Islam was conversant with the practice, there is also ample evidence that shabd and nad yoga constituted one of the key practices employed by nirguna bhakti poets in the Sant tradition and later by the Sikh gurus in North India (Barthwal 1978).

Kabir (1440–1518), for instance, perhaps the most well-known and celebrated Sant, speaks at length about meditating on the inner sound.

Day and night, the celestial bugles vibrate the unstruck melody. Then, one beholds the Father of the three worlds.

There the Unstruck Music is sounded; it is the music of the love of the three worlds. There millions of lamps of sun and of moon are burning; there the drum beats, and the lover swings in play. There love-songs resound, and light rains in showers; and the worshipper is entranced in the taste of the heavenly nectar. (Tagore 2016: 30, 32)

The Sikh holy scriptures, Sri Guru Granth Sahib, are full of references from various Sants/Bhagats, including Ravidas, Farid, Surdas, and Jaidev. Although the teachings of these mystics vary in parts, there are common themes around bhakti, high moral living, and meditating on the inner sound.

Guru Nanak (1469–1539), the founder of Sikhism, and his nine successors laid great stress on nam and shabd.

Various are the unending dulcet Melodies, one cannot describe their delicious strains.

The glorious consummation takes place, when the Lord of the five Melodies comes.

The wondrous Music of the five melodies, God Himself may make audible if He so wisheth. (K. Singh 2017: 250–57)

The contentious issue that is still debated among Sikhs and those reading their holy scriptures is how best to interpret what shabd means. Does listening to five inner sounds really capture the essence of Nanak's and Arjan's religious insights?

This controversy over hermeneutics is not unique to Sikhism, since the same question arises in Hindu, Buddhist, Christian, and Muslim circles. Those who are inclined to view spiritual practice as an internal quest – not necessarily conforming to orthodox theology – tend to see references to sound and light as having a mystical and experiential import, whereas those who opt for more literalistic and communal explanations discount such personal revelation – sometimes accusing those of a mystical orientation of being heretical in their views and practices (Berger 1979). We have seen this type of conflict in Christianity over the issue of glossolalia, where some have argued that genuine speaking in tongues only occurred among the apostles two millennia ago and that modern manifestations of the phenomenon, as it occurs among Pentecostals, is merely imitative or due to emotional hysteria (Goodman 2008).

Much of the tension revolves around questions of authority and who is best equipped or accepted to adjudicate such metaphysical matters. This conflict arises again and again in new religious movements, which in their desire to achieve uniqueness or superiority over their rival counterparts will speak of higher and lower levels of shabd access and initiation. Peter Berger suggests that religion can be viewed from three distinct perspectives: deductive, reductive, and inductive. In simple parlance: (1) believers hold that their respective religion is true by virtue of a revelation that cannot be doubted; (2) skeptics argue that religion is illusory because it cannot hold up to rational scrutiny; and (3) one must keep an open mind about the truth or falsity of religion, which warrants further unbiased investigation (Berger 1979).

Berger's schema can also serve as a template by which to view shabd yoga-related movements – ranging from those who firmly hold that the sound current is divine, to those who believe it is purely neurological in origin (tinnitus?), to those who are essentially agnostic about its origination and are open to further inquiry.

What further complicates these disputations is a strong belief that the shabd and the spiritual master are one and that access to the sound current depends upon the conscious transmission or grace of one's initiating guru. Without such a formal initiation into the shabd yoga practice, the neophyte will not have access to the higher frequencies of the sound current and thus his or her upward ascent will be sidetracked. Kirpal Singh, founder of Ruhani Satsang, in a response to a questioner concerning initiation, said the following:

> Initiation by a perfect Living Master assures an escort in unknown realms by One who is Himself a frequent traveler to those regions. He knows the

presiding deities or powers of the planes, conducts the spirit step by step, counsels at every turn and twist of the Path, cautions against lurking dangers at each place, explaining in detail all that one desires to know. He is a teacher on all levels of existence; a Guru on the earth-plane, a Guru Dev (Astral Radiant Form) in the Astral Worlds and a Satguru in the purely Spiritual Regions. When everyone fails in this very life, at one stage or another, His long and strong arm is always there to help us, both when we are here and [when] we quit the earth plane. He pilots the spirit into the Beyond and stands by it, even before the judgment seat of God. (K. Singh 1967: 52)

It is therefore not surprising that perceived masters of shabd yoga are accorded a very high status and seekers wishing to learn more about the technique invariably must follow certain guidelines in order to receive initiation and learn the secret techniques about the practice.

The Radhasoami Tradition

This point comes into sharper focus when we look at modern sound current movements, starting with the Radhasoami tradition, which has had an enormous influence on new religious movements that advocate listening to the sound current as an essential feature of their teachings. What we will see is how a simple technique gets intricately intertwined with guru politics and theology (Juergensmeyer 1991; Lane 1992; Kaushal 1998).

By the mid-nineteenth century in North India, the Sant tradition had made a significant impact on a number of emerging new religious groups, including the Kabir-panthis, Satnamis, and Sikh-related sects such as the Namdharis and Nirankaris (McLeod & Schomer 1987).

One of the more significant movements to have emerged from Santism is the Radhasoami tradition as founded by Shiv Dayal Singh (1818–1878). His family was closely associated with Sikhism, though not formally part of the Khalsa. They were great admirers of Guru Nanak and his teachings. According to the *Biography of Soamiji Maharaj*, written two decades later by his youngest brother, Pratap Singh, their parents were devotees of Tulsi Sahib of Hathras, whose teachings were closely aligned with those of Kabir, Nanak, Paltu Sahib, and Dariya Sahib (P. Singh 1978).

Tulsi Sahib taught shabd yoga and it appears obvious, even if contested in certain orthodox quarters of Radhsoami, that he instructed Shiv Dayal Singh, more popularly known as Soamiji Maharaj, into the technique of listening to the inner sound current. This method was threefold: (1) repetition of sacred name/ names, (2) contemplation of the initiating guru or light within, and (3) listening to inner sounds. There are also reports that one of Tulsi Sahib's successors, Girdhari Das, was regarded as a guru by Shiv Dayal Singh and treated with the respect accorded to a Mahatma. It may well be that Girdhari also helped groom and guide Soamiji Maharaj after Tulsi Sahib's death in 1843, since the founder of Radhasoami did not announce his satsang publicly until 1861, several months *after* Girdhari's death in July 1860. James Bean has done extensive research in connecting Shiv Dayal Singh's tutelage under Girdhari Das, illustrating for the first time how intimate and prolonged the relationship was between these two gurus after the death of Tulsi Sahib in Hathras (Bean 2017).

It is remarkable to note that a small spiritual movement founded in the mid-nineteenth century would over time have a worldwide impact on the practice of shabd yoga. This has occurred primarily because the Radhasoami tradition has blossomed into a large number of distinct branches throughout India and abroad. These same groups have in turn witnessed further splintering and there has been a surprising contingent of new religious movements such as Eckankar, MasterPath, MSIA, and Quan Yin, that, though distancing themselves from a direct lineal connection to Radhasoami, owe a large debt to Shiv Dayal Singh and his successors. Much of this is due to the clarity with which various Radhasoami masters have explained the path of surat shabd yoga. The modernization of shabd yoga is due largely to Shiv Dayal Singh's core text, *Sar Bachan*, both prose and poetry, which was first published in Hindi in 1884 and subsequently translated into several languages, including English. Furthermore, the numerous writings from his main successor, Rai Salig Ram, particularly *Radhasoami Mat Prakash* (1896), were also instrumental in popularizing these hitherto esoteric teachings.. Later gurus in both the Agra and Beas branches published extensively in English, Hindi, Urdu, and Punjabi (Lane 2018a).

Professor Andrea Diem-Lane's book *The Guru in America* (2015) offers several explanations for why Soamiji Maharaji's message carried beyond the parochial confines of Agra. Besides the dissemination of his teachings in various publications by later successors, one innovation that was instrumental was allowing initiation by proxy. Soamiji allowed certain designated disciples to give his technical instructions on meditation in outlying areas in which they were living or visiting. After his death some of his spiritual heirs printed the instructions and had them conveyed by mail.

Diem-Lane further argues that the expansion of communicative technologies and their acceptance is elemental for any new religion to have an impact.

> The evolution of religion is directly connected to the evolution of communication technologies. To understand the limits of the latter is to also understand the limits of the former's potential for growth. . . . The history of Radhasoami in the United States is a case in point. Why? Because in many ways the growth of Radhasoami in countries outside of India has been hitched, for better or worse, to the advancement of technology. . . . At each stage where

there has been a technological revolution, there has been in turn an influx of new initiates to the Radhasoami path. (Diem-Lane 2015: 17)

Soamiji's total initiates were just several thousand during his lifetime, but in the century and a half after his death the number of Radhasoami followers has increased exponentially. Today the Radha Soami Satsang at Beas alone claims to have five thousand centers throughout India and nearly one hundred worldwide. This is quite remarkable when one realizes that this number doesn't include the other more than thirty different Radhasoami branches and all of their respective initiates. Although an exact tally is not yet possible, it is generally estimated that there are more than five to six million followers of Radhasoami worldwide (Juergensmeyer 1991; Kaushal 1998; Lane 2018b).

Much of this increase is due to the continual splintering off of rival factions within Radhasoami, which allowed for a multiplicity of gurus – each with his/her own modern center – to spread the teachings in new and innovative ways. Moreover, several of these same shabd yoga masters began to travel throughout India and eventually abroad to Europe and North America, attracting Westerners who were unfamiliar with the teachings but who were nevertheless attracted to the simplicity and power of shabd yoga.

In addition, several books on Radhasoami and listening to the inner sound current became popular and were widely read. Outstanding among these texts and one title that still sells thousands of copies yearly is Julian Phillip Johnson's *The Path of the Masters*, which was first published in 1939 shortly after the author's untimely death at the hands of mountaineer Paul Petzoldt (Lane 2017a). This book, as well as his earlier publication *With a Great Master in India* (1934), was written in a clear and accessible style and spoke of "great masters" who had the secrets to unlock the riddle of existence. Both books served as beacons for attracting new followers to Radhasoami. Ironically, they were also widely plagiarized and judicious excerpts were incorporated into the teachings of other new religious movements, such as Doctor Bhagat Singh Thind's study groups and Paul Twitchell's Eckankar (Lane 1983).

Another book that introduced shabd yoga teachings worldwide was Paul Brunton's *A Search in Secret India*, first published in 1934, which contained a whole chapter devoted to the Radhasoami center at Dayalbagh in Agra. Brunton writes glowingly of its leader at the time, Anand Swarup (Sahabji Maharaj [1881–1937]), who was the successor of Kamta P. Sinha (1871–1913) from Ghazipur, and questions whether the inner sound current heard during meditation is not the result of one's own nervous system. The discussion he has with the Dayalbagh master still resonates today.

Sahabji: But the basis of them is "Sound-Yoga," or "listening for the internal sound," as we usually call it.

Brunton: The writings I am studying say that sound is the force which called the universe into being.

Sahabji: From a material standpoint you understand it correctly, but rather it is that a current of sound was the first activity of the Supreme Being at the beginning of creation. The universe is not the result of blind forces. Now this divine sound is known to our fraternity and can be phonetically transcribed. It is our belief that sounds bear the impress of their source, of the power which created them. Therefore, when one of our members listens internally and expectantly for the divine sound, with controlled body, mind and will, he will become lifted up towards the bliss and wisdom of the Supreme Being as soon as he hears the divine sound.

Brunton: Is it not possible to imagine that the sound of the blood beating through one's arteries is the divine sound? What other sound can one hear internally?

Sahabji: Ah, we do not mean any material sound, but a spiritual one. The force which appears as sound on our material plane is only a reflection of that subtler force whose workings evolved the universe. (Brunton 1985: 242–45)

Today it is estimated that at least thirty Radhasoami-related movements – each with its own leader and separate organization – have a significant outreach around the world, particularly in Europe, Australia, Africa, and North and South America.

1. Radhasoami Satsang Dayalbagh, Agra

Of all the Radhasoami movements, the Dayalbagh Satsang in Agra, India, is the one most focused on studying shabd yoga from a scientific perspective (Sriamamurti, Prashant & Mohan 2013). The current spiritual leader, Prem Saran Satsangi (b. 1934), is a highly trained electrical engineer who has sponsored a wide range of academic conferences for the express purpose of better understanding the neurobiological basis of human consciousness. The Dayalbagh Educational Institute in Agra has published a number of technical reports on how listening to the inner sound current can have a positive impact on the brain and the extended nervous system. Perhaps unique among all of the Radhasoami groups, Dayalbagh has invited distinguished physicists, philosophers, and neuroscientists from around the world to present their latest research findings in order to unravel the mystery of self-awareness. Such notable thinkers include Sir Roger Penrose, the 2020 Nobel Prize winner in physics, Leonard Mlodinow from California Institute of Technology, and Craig Hogan, the director of the Fermilab Center for Particle Astrophysics at the University of Chicago.

One model that Dayalbagh has strongly advocated was developed by Prem Saran Satsangi. It is called TEASE: "Towards Evolutionary Arts, Science, and Engineering of Consciousness." After many years of development, it centers on an "Omni-quantum theory for spiritual consciousness system modelling in cosmology" (Dayalbagh Educational Institute 2021). The goal is a greater appreciation of how inner experiences gained through deep meditation on the sound current can transform our understanding of how the universe operates. The Dayalbagh Educational Institute essentially views cosmology through the lens of Radhasoami teachings and believes that science and religion are not intrinsic enemies.

In this regard, the practice of shabd yoga is viewed as a fundamental necessity in order to unravel nature's hidden teleological underpinnings. In other words, "Rather than soaring into space in search of macrocosmic secrets, one turns inward and discovers the secrets, otherwise not revealed in the world outside" (Dayalbagh Educational Institute 2021).

2. Radha Soami Satsang Beas

The Beas branch of Radhasoami, which has chosen to spell the words Radha and Soami separately in contradistinction with the Agra satsangs, was established by Jaimal Singh (1839–1903), a soldier in the Indian-British army who permanently retired on the banks of the Beas river in 1889, which he chose for his residence since it was quite secluded and would provide an ideal location for prolonged meditation (K. Singh 1960). His main successor, Sawan Singh (1858–1948), developed a large center in honor of his guru and today, under the leadership of Gurinder Singh (b. 1954), it has become the largest Radhasoami group in the world with millions of followers. It now has centers in ninety countries across the globe (Juergensmeyer 1991; Kapur 1994; Kaushal 1998). Like other Radhasoami-related satsangs, they advocate a threefold meditational process: (1) simran, repetition of five names; (2) dhyan, contemplation on the guru or the light within; and (3) bhajan, listening to the inner sound (C. Singh 1999). The Beas Satsang has published an extensive number of books in forty languages, with English being their most popular idiom. In the United States alone they have built ten large properties for holding satsang. When the guru makes his semiannual visits, there can be well over four thousand people in attendance, though the vast majority of attendees are from an Indian background. The early appeal of Radhasoami to Westerners has clearly waned since its peak in the 1980s during Charan Singh's (1916–1990) tenure. While the number of Indians seeking initiation at Beas from the current guru, Gurinder Singh, has witnessed steady growth, the number of Westerners without an Indian familial connection has dropped precipitously. Sociologically speaking, this is most likely due to a number of factors, including the continual number of guru scandals both in India and abroad, the heightened interest in new technologies, and a growing disdain for authoritarian leadership.

The Beas Satsang has gone to great lengths to explain that shabd yoga is not unique to India and can be found in almost all of the world's religions. In this regard they have published twenty-five volumes in their Mysticism in the World series, replete with such titles as *Yoga and the Bible* (1971), *The Mystic Heart of Judaism* (2011), and *Buddhism: Path to Nirvana* (Upadhyaya 2010). A group of evangelical Christians visiting the Dera at Beas interviewed Charan Singh and asked him, "What is this teaching that all the mystics of the world teach?" To which he responded:

> Our spiritual journey starts from the eye center, upward. So we have to withdraw our consciousness back to the eye center. And after that you have to travel with that light and sound within. That is why Christ said, "If your eye is single, your whole body is full of light." We have to open this eye and see that light. With the help of that light, we have to find our way back to God. Christ said that spiritual worship pleases the Father. And that Spirit, that Holy Ghost, that Word, that Logos that is in every one of us is here at the eye center. Indian mystics have given Indian names, Christ has given his own name, Persian mystics have given their own name, but those who have travelled within on that path, they have the same message to give. They are not bound by any ritual, by any ceremonies; they don't have anything to worship outside of themselves, they only worship Him within. (Lane 2016b: 6)

Radhasoami's attempt to find the sound current teachings sprinkled throughout all of the world's major religions has inspired splinter groups to emphasize the same. Because of this, the novel idea of shabd yoga can be more appealing to those who have never entertained such a concept or technique before. However, it must be acknowledged that devout followers of these very religions don't necessarily agree with Radhasoami's interpretation of their respective holy books or doctrines. This has led biblical scholars such as John Robinson (1919–1983) to take issue with Radhasoami's gnostic view of the New Testament, particularly refashioning such phrases as "If your eye be single, your whole body is full of light" to be indicative of the "third eye" and deep meditation. Thus Robinson, no doubt with a bit of irony, entitled his book *Truth Is Two-Eyed* (1979).

3. The Ruhani Satsang Influence

After the death of his guru, Sawan Singh, Kirpal Singh (1894–1974) founded Ruhani Satsang in Delhi, India. Although he discarded the name Radhasoami as a descriptive moniker for his group, he completely aligned his movement with his teacher, Sawan Singh, and his predecessors. Indeed Kirpal Singh argued that he was part of an unbroken lineage of gurus that went back through Shiv Dayal Singh to the ten Sikh gurus, starting with Guru Nanak. Kirpal suggests that the tenth Sikh guru, Gobind Singh, transferred his mastership to Ratnagar Rao, who in turn passed the mantle to Tulsi Sahib of Hathras. The problem with the theory, however, is that there is no historical evidence that such a Ratnagar Rao ever existed. Moreover, Kirpal Singh's attempt to tie his movement with the Sikhs discounts the core doctrine among Sikhs worldwide that Gobind Singh designated a holy book, Sri Guru Granth Sahib, as the final guru (K. Singh 1960; Lane 2017b; Tessler 2017). By doing such, Kirpal was underlining why his ministry is a continuation of the Sant tradition and that his teachings were no different than what the ten Sikh gurus taught. Kirpal Singh emphasized that when he gave initiation to new disciples they would have a firsthand experience of light and sound during their meditation sitting. This was a compelling advertisement for his group and has been mimicked by all of his reputed successors since his death in 1974. It is now a common theme among gurus in Kirpal Singh's lineage that anyone receiving initiation should have a personal experience of light and sound during the ceremony. Kirpal's innovation was not entirely new since Partap Singh declares that his older brother, Shiv Dayal Singh, the founder of Radhasoami, "often used to raise a little the spirit of certain Adhikaris (fitted and deserving) at the time of initiation. Thus, they had a foretaste of the bliss of higher regions and developed faith instantly" (P. Singh 1978: 23).

Kirpal Singh conducted three tours to North America, in 1955, 1963, and 1972, with each new visit witnessing an exponential increase in the number of attendees. Kirpal Singh also published a number of widely read books that introduced the concept of the sound current to thousands worldwide. These texts include *Crown of Life* (1973), *Night Is a Jungle* (1975), and *Naam or Word* (1974). Each provides a wealth of information on the practice of shabd yoga in various traditions and was instrumental in spreading the practice of listening to the inner sound current. Kirpal Singh initiated eighty thousand disciples during his lifetime.

After Kirpal Singh's death came a severe succession crisis that resulted in a plethora of successors, with each claiming to be the rightful heir. These included Kirpal Singh's eldest son, Darshan Singh (1921–1989), who eventually gathered the largest following and established Sawan-Kirpal Mission. He was succeeded by his eldest son, Rajinder Singh (b. 1946), who retained his residence in Chicago, Illinois, and who has made significant strides in making shabd yoga more accessible to a Westernized audience via his Science of Spirituality organization. Thakar Singh (1929–2005) was appointed by Madam Hardevi, a longtime associate of Kirpal Singh and the chief administrator of Sawan Ashram. He created a center in Umpqua, Oregon, which is now called the Lighthouse and serves as a meditation retreat. Before Thakar died he appointed Baljit Singh (b. 1962) as his successor. Baljit Singh has carried on the ministry under the name "Know Thyself As Soul." The organization has twenty-five centers scattered throughout the United States and offers initiation in its version of Sant Mat. Ajaib Singh (1926–1997) became known in the West when he was discovered by Arran Stephens of Vancouver, Canada, and later supported by Russell Perkins, who was well known because of Sant Bani ashram and press in Sanbornton, New Hampshire. His following was never very large, numbering several thousand, and those who claimed succession after him, such as Sadhu Ram (b. 1944) and Ram Singh (b. 1954), have kept a relatively low profile.

Primarily because Kirpal Singh and several of those who followed in his lineage, particularly Rajinder Singh, have not disdained advertising, they have made the practice of listening to the inner sound current much more widely known than in decades past. Unquestionably, Kirpal Singh and the various organizations that have emerged from his teachings are responsible to a large degree for why shabd yoga is no longer an obscure topic of discussion among spiritual seekers (Lane 1992).

4. Ishwar Puri and the Institute for the Study of Human Awareness (ISHA)

The emergence of new shabd yoga movements usually follows a predictable pattern. Whenever a guru appoints a bona fide successor, inevitably after the guru dies – with few exceptions – there will be disciples who believe that they should be the rightful heir apparent or have a designated role to carry on their master's teachings. Such students typically proclaim their particular calling within a few months after their teacher's departure. Others, however, may wait years to come out publicly. Ishwar Puri (1926–2020) is a good example of the latter. Although he founded the Institute for the Study of Human Awareness (ISHA) as a nonprofit organization in the 1960s, he was not viewed then as a spiritual master. Rather Puri was closely aligned with Radha Soami Satsang Beas and its leader at the time, Charan Singh. Indeed Puri was a popular satsang speaker for the group for many years. Puri was only nine years old in the mid-1930s when he was initiated by Charan's grandfather Sawan Singh at Beas. His father and extended family were all closely aligned with Sawan Singh and his later successors. Ishwar Puri was a high-ranking government official in the Punjab for many years. After settling in America, he did graduate work at Harvard University and served as a consultant to several businesses. Decades after his own guru's death in 1948 Puri began giving initiation as a seva to his own master to seekers who sought him out as a spiritual master, though he tended to downplay his own status when directly asked about such in public.

This led to him becoming more active in developing his own organization and giving talks around the country. Accordingly Puri would grant initiation in the name of his own master each year on April 2, on the anniversary of the death of his guru, Sawan Singh.

Because a large number of Ishwar Puri's talks were featured on YouTube, he became much more popular during the last ten years of his life. His organization, though relatively small, began building a center in Bruce, Wisconsin, that would eventually house a large auditorium with a seating capacity of four hundred and later a much bigger facility.

Due to Ishwar Puri's death from COVID-19 on December 23, 2020, there has been some controversy over who should serve as his spiritual successor or if he actually named anyone to succeed him. Presently several candidates are vying for the position, including Dwight Samuels, who explained his own nomination in his book entitled *The Seeker and the Sought* (Samuels 2020).

Puri's teachings dovetail almost point by point with other Radhasoami groups concerning the importance of listening to the inner sound current. In response to an email question, Puri explained the importance of shabd.

> The real sound that pulls us out of our body comes from within ourselves which in the wakeful state is at the eye center. When that sound pulls us we lose awareness of right ear or left ear as we ascend to a higher state of consciousness where we get actual experiences of our Astral self. The resounding bell sound does not come from any side. It is a sound that surrounds us because it is coming from within us. (Puri 2022)

Puri goes on to explain that the reason so many traditions, particularly Sant Mat and Radhasoami, lay emphasis on shabd is that it allows one to detach from the world and its pleasures. He elaborated in a response to a questioner. "The constant sound can appear as early as the attention gathering around the third eye. However, the constant sound keeps changing as we move up from level to level of higher Consciousness! As the attention gets more and more attached to the Sound one experiences more and more of detachment from this world" (Puri 2022).

Because Ishwar Puri and his followers have published more than two hundred and fifty distinct filmed recordings of his talks on the Internet, his teachings are garnering a wide audience even after his death.

In following the spread of shabd yoga teachings on new religious movements in North America and elsewhere, it is necessary to genealogically identify where, when, and how different Indian schools of thought produced such an influence. Thus, in describing the following new religions, we want to document as much as possible how certain core ideas and practices are adopted and transformed over time.

The Sound Current Tradition in the West

1. Helena Blavatsky and Theosophy

One of the most remarkable aspects about Theosophy, as founded by Helena Petrovna Blavatsky (1831–1891), in 1875 in New York City, is that it rekindled a great interest among middle- and upper-class Indians in their own traditions, from which many were drifting away due to the influence of capitalism, Christianity, and modern science (Garrett 1895; Cranston 1993; Meade 2014). Theosophy also generated tremendous enthusiasm for all things Eastern among Americans and Europeans. Blavatsky wrote prodigiously about fusing occult teachings (drawn from her wide readings in Hinduism and Buddhism) with modern science. Although critics dismissed much of her work as either unreadable or pseudoscientific, her admirers praised her literary skill in bringing esotericism to the masses.

One of her most popular books was the *The Voice of the Silence*, originally published in 1889, which provides a distillation of sound current teachings. Blavatsky alleges that she translated the text from "The Book of Golden Precepts" and provides a rather convoluted explanation behind its origin in her preface.

> The original Precepts are engraved on thin oblong squares; copies very often on discs. These discs, or plates, are generally preserved on the altars of the temples attached to centres where the so-called "contemplative" or Mahâyâna (Yogâchâra) schools are established. They are written variously, sometimes in Tibetan but mostly in ideographs. The sacerdotal language (Senzar), besides an alphabet of its own, may be rendered in several modes of writing in cypher characters, which partake more of the nature of ideographs than of syllables. (Blavatsky 2015: vii)

Regardless of the book's true origination – though both the Dalai Lama and D. T. Suzuki have acknowledged its Mahayana Buddhist influence – it does present the teachings of the sound current in a hierarchical fashion that is reminiscent of the *Nadabindu Upanishad*, *Hatha Yoga Pradipika*, and the Sant, Sufi, and Radhasoami traditions. The following list, which we have gleaned from the four distinct traditions, provides a comparative overview.

THE VOICE OF THE SILENCE

1. Nightingale's sweet voice chanting
2. Silver cymbal
3. Ocean sprite imprisoned in its shell [conch]
4. Vina
5. Bamboo flute
6. Trumpet blast
7. Rumbling of a thundercloud

NADABINDU UPANISHAD

1. Mardala/drums
2. Bell
3. Horn
4. Tinkling bells
5. Flute
6. Vina
7. Bees

HATHA YOGA PRADIPIKA

1. Beating/jingling drums
2. Conch, Mridanga, bells
3. Tinklets, flute, Vina, bees

RADHASOAMI TRADITION

1. Bells
2. Conch
3. Sarangi
4. Flute
5. Vina

Intriguingly, there is historical evidence that Blavatsky was aware of the Radhasoami tradition and its sound current teachings as far back as the 1880s, if not prior, since Alfred Percy Sinnett's (1840–1921) book *The Occult World* (1881) mentions Rai Salig Ram (1829–1898), the chief disciple and successor of Shiv Dayal Singh, the founder of Radhasoami. Blavatsky and Henry Steel Olcott (1832–1907), the cofounder of Theosophy, postulated that there were

"Masters of the Hidden Brotherhood" (Juergensmeyer 1991). These enlightened Mahatmas from Tibet were alleged to have communicated their insights directly to Sinnett through a series of letters. The idea that such correspondence was possible came from Blavatsky, who encouraged Sinnett in his mission to find answers to his many spiritual questions.

While Hare and Hare (1936) systematically argued that these letters were a literary fraud, the letters do nevertheless reveal actual historical events and persons, which provides a rich resource to better trace the source material from which many Theosophical ideas were drawn.

K. Paul Johnson in his book *The Masters Revealed* (1994) goes so far as to suggest that Blavatsky employed cover names such as Master Koot Hoomi and Master Morya for those gurus and yogis with whom she had actually come in contact. Blavatsky constructed a mythology of her own making, but one that was at least partially based on real-life events and personages.

In letter thirty-one of the *Mahatma Letters* (1923) the following passage explicitly mentions Rai Salig Ram and his philosophy, though clearly trying to show the inferiority of his system – Radhasoami – and that of his initiating guru, Shiv Dayal Singh, to those of the Theosophical masters.

> Suby Ram [Salig Ram] – a truly good man – yet a devotee of another error. Not his guru's voice – his own. The voice of a pure, unselfish, earnest soul, absorbed in misguided, misdirected mysticism. Add to it a chronic disorder in that portion of the brain which responds to clear vision and the secret is soon told: that disorder was developed by forced visions; by hatha yog [*sic*] and prolonged asceticism. S. Ram is the chief medium and at same time the principal magnetic factor, who spreads his disease by infection – unconsciously to himself; who inoculates with his vision all the other disciples. There is one general law of vision (physical and mental or spiritual) but there is a qualifying special law proving that all vision must be determined by the quality or grade of man's spirit and soul, and also by the ability to translate divers qualities of waves of astral light into consciousness. There is but one general law of life, but innumerable laws qualify and determine the myriads of forms perceived and of sounds heard. There are those who are willingly and others who are unwillingly – blind.
>
> (Sinnett 1923: 255–56)

Daniel Caldwell, a longtime follower of Theosophy and an expert on its early history, discovered that a close reading of the original letter to Sinnett was wrongly transcribed. Instead of Suby Ram, it actually was Salig Ram. Moreover, the society that is referenced is the Radhasoami movement as founded by Salig Ram's guru, Shiv Dayal Singh. It appears that Sinnett was interested in the teaching of Radhasoami and that the letter from the Mahatma Morya was a three-layered critique against Salig Ram, his guru, and the visionary claims made by the tradition, which is labeled "disease by infection." Daniel Caldwell writes, "It would appear that in the latter part of 1881, Sinnett had met Rai Salig Ram in Allahabad. Salig Ram told Sinnett about his deceased guru Shiv Dayal Singh. Sinnett, who was at the same time in correspondence with Madame Blavatsky's teachers, wrote to Master Morya inquiring about Shiv Dayal Singh, Rai Salig Ram and their claims" (Caldwell 2004: 2).

What is curious here, however, is that the sound current teachings of Blavatsky's *The Voice of the Silence* and those of Salig Ram are quite similar, though the Mahatma letters provide no indication of that. It is worthwhile noting that Salig Ram was himself a subscriber to the *Theosophist*, a monthly magazine published in Adyar, India.

Because *The Voice of the Silence* was one of Theosophy's most popular publications and is still in print, it has continually introduced shabd/nad yoga to thousands and is a common resource for a number of new religious movements. The present Dalai Lama reportedly stated that "I believe that [*The Voice of the Silence*] has strongly influenced many sincere seekers and aspirants to the wisdom and compassion of the Bodhisattva Path" (Theosociety 2022). It has also served as instructive material to many not associated with any Indian and Tibetan religion. For example, Maurice Wilson, the World War I veteran and legendary would-be mountaineer of Mount Everest, referred to Blavatsky's tome as the one spiritual text that guided him more than any other in his life (Caesar 2020).

2. Paramahansa Yogananda and the Self-Realization Fellowship

Since Swami Vivekananda (1863–1902) introduced Vedanta at the World's Parliament of Religions in Chicago in 1893 and was warmly received (Nivedita 1910), there has been a continual influx of visiting swamis and yogis. In 1920 Paramahansa Yogananda (1893–1952) came to America and over time his Self-Realization Fellowship (SRF) became well established in the United States, with two large centers in Los Angeles and Encinitas, California. His book, *Autobiography of a Yogi* (Yogananda 1946), became extremely popular after his death in 1952 and introduced thousands to his version of kriya yoga.

One key teaching in the SRF is the "Aum technique of meditation." This is a practice where the aspirant plugs both ears and focuses on listening to the inner sound. The official SRF website explains:

> These astral sounds are likened to melodic strains of the humming of a bee, the tone of a flute, a stringed instrument such as a harp, a bell-like or gong

sound, the soothing roar of a distant sea, and a cosmic symphony of all vibratory sound. The Self-Realization Fellowship technique of meditation on Aum teaches one to hear and locate these astral sounds. This aids the awakening of the divine consciousness locked in the spinal centers, opening them to "make straight" the way of ascension to God-realization.

(Yogananda.org 2022)

In India the neophyte is taught a specific version of the malasana posture, which is essentially squatting and resting the elbows on the knees and then using the right and left thumbs to plug each ear. Another alternative that has gained popularity both in India and abroad is the baragon (beragon/barragon) or T-stick, which in the SRF is known as the "Aum Board" or meditation armrest. The purpose, of course, is to minimize outside noises so that it is easier to listen to subtle sounds within.

The intriguing historical question revolves around when, where, and how Yogananda learned of shabd or nad yoga. According to Swami Satyananda Giri, a follower of both Sri Yukestwar and Yogananda, when Mukunda (Yogananda's birth name) was a young boy he learned the practice of nad yoga from a family acquaintance. Charu Babu was a follower of Radhasoami and he personally told Yogananda when he was just a boy the secret technique that is given at the time of initiation. As Giri explains, "The sharp young Mukunda engaged himself in sadhana with full mind and heart and in a very short duration of time he was able to hear the 'Nada' (divine sound) and perceived the 'Apurba Dibya Jyoti' (divine light) and was overwhelmed" (Giri 2021: 20).

In addition, Yogananda's own guru, Sri Yukestwar from Serampore, was quite conversant with the yoga of the inner sound current. His only published book in English, *The Holy Science* (1957), describes the ancient practice and even labels it as "surat sabda yoga." Writes Yukestwar:

It will be found how a disciple, while passing through the different stages, becomes able to conceive the different objects of creation in his heart, and how he gradually advances to the state of meditation, and ultimately by concentrating his attention to the sensorium, he perceives the peculiar sound Pranava or Sabda the holy word, when the heart becomes divine, and the Ego, Ahankara or the Son of Man, becomes merged or baptised in the stream thereof and the disciple becomes siddha, an adept Divine personage.

(Yukteswar 2020)

There are several yoga schools that teach kriya yoga and that are distinct from the SRF, but that share Yogananda's spiritual lineage of gurus from Sri Yukestwar to Lahiri Mahayasa to the mysterious Babaji, the alleged ancient founder (Lane 2020b). These groups include Swami Kriyananda's Ananda

Yoga movement (Kriyananda 1988) and Paramahamsa Hariharananda's Kriya Yoga International (Hariharananda 1992), each of which also includes sound current meditation as part of its teachings.

3. Prem Rawat and the Divine Light Mission

Although the Divine Light Mission, as originally founded by Hans Ram Singh Rawat (1900–1966), has undergone several transformations after his son, Prem Rawat (b. 1957), succeeded his father when he was only eight years old, the core teaching that was propounded was that of shabd yoga. Hans Ram Singh Rawat was an initiate of Beli Ram, honorifically known as Shri Swami Swarupanand Ji Maharaj (1884–1936), who was the second guru in the spiritual lineage of Advait Mat. There are unverified reports that Hans Ram Singh Rawat also took initiation from Sawan Singh of Radha Soami Satsang Beas, as reported by Kirpal Singh's secretary, Gyaniji, who provided this information when interviewed at Sawan Ashram in Delhi, India, in June 1978 (Lane 1983).

The teachings of this tradition, as founded by Ram Yaad (Shri Paramhans Swami Advaitanand Ji Maharaj), are a modern version of Sant Mat, as its adherents readily admit in their literature, making connections to previous Sants such as Kabir. The following excerpts from *Shri Paramhans Advait Mat* (Anandpur Trust 1975) provide a glimpse of their philosophy:

> To set right the troubled conditions of the world by imparting spiritual knowledge and Bhakti' to the people, to arrange the spiritual advancement through Surat-Shabad Yoga (Yoga of sound and light); to show the path of Sewa' all this composed in one noble and high ideal is called Sant Mat' in the common parlance. Sant Mat' is the means to acquire spirituality and Bhakti. The saints are free from enmity, jealousy and rivalry. They are impartial and sympathetic to all. They uplift all, without distinction, through their nectarean teachings. The "Vadas," the "Shastras" and the "Granthas" have confirmed it. The great spiritualists, while accepting this eternal truth, have said that they do not come to form a new sect or religion, but only to show the path, indicated earlier by the great reincarnations and the saints. This path is also called the path of "Surat-Shabad-Yoga." The human beings, having been caught in the snare of Kaal' and Maya' (death and illusion) since innumerable births and, thus, separated from the Lord have been a victim of worries. To unite the conscious with the Master and to unite the soul with God is the lofty ideal of Sant Mat'. (Anandpur Trust 1975: 28)

The Divine Light Mission underwent a dramatic transformation in the early 1980s when Prem Rawat disbanded the ashram infrastructure of the organization and altered the direction of his movement to become less overtly religious and more modernized. He also altered the name eventually to Elan Vital and focused his activities less on his godlike guru status as such, and more as a philanthropic organization known as "The Prem Rawat Foundation," which is designed to promote "dignity, peace, and prosperity by addressing the fundamental human needs of food, water, and peace." Critics, however, have raised questions about Prem Rawat's intentions since much of the donated money is used to support his expensive lifestyle.

Those taking initiation would receive the "Knowledge" that Prem Rawat offered – usually through a series of appointed designees originally called Mahatmas – and were given a fourfold meditation technique: (1) light, where one focuses on the proverbial third eye; (2) music, where the aspirant plugs each ear and tries to listen to the sound current; (3) word, which is a pranayama technique where one becomes conscious of a certain breathing pattern and the sound of soham (sohung/sohang); and (4) nectar, which is a modified version of a yogic practice known as kechari mudra, where the tongue is placed at the back of the throat near the nasal passage. The official Prem Rawat website provides background about the evolution of this community and its teachings:

> According to his followers, Shri Hans was early in his life an egalitarian iconoclast, and an opponent of the Hindu caste system. He was originally a member of the Arya Samaj, but left that movement after he met a guru of the Sant Mat tradition, Sri Swarupanand Ji Maharaj. Swarupanand initiated him into the four techniques of Knowledge or kriyas, which are the centrepiece of his religion. In the 1930s following the death of his guru, he began to travel in Sind and Lahore and later to Delhi.
>
> (Prem Rawat official website 2022)

Much of the knowledge that Prem Rawat and his father passed on appears derived, at least in part, from the early yogic manual the *Gheranda Samhita* (Mallinson 2004), since each of the four techniques that they imparted are mentioned in the text, particularly connecting inhaling and exhaling breath with soham: "The breath of every person in entering makes the sound of 'sah' and in coming out, that of 'ham.' These two sounds make (so' ham 'I am That') or (hamsa 'The Great Swan')" (Dudeja 2018: 198).

As for the importance of shabd/nad in the Divine Light Mission in the early days, one disciple explained it thusly. "The mahatma directs you to sit with your thumbs in your ears and your elbows propped up on a wooden board called a braggan. They tell you to concentrate on one of your ears. You begin to hear sounds. Your body makes subtle little noises, your heart and your blood swishing around – it makes noise and that's what you hear. You have to do it in a really quiet room. Your powers of concentration increase with practice of the techniques. It's really a trip; your body's out-of-sight, it makes all these far-out noises and you can really get into it" (Prem Rawat Biography 2022).

Prem Rawat has modified this "Knowledge" over the past few decades, though his use of the term dates back to his father's own usage, which he himself learned from his association with Beli Ram and the Advait Mat teachings (Anandpur Trust 1975).

4. Dr. Bhagat Singh Thind and Spiritual Science

Bhagat Singh Thind (1892–1967) was born a Sikh and attended Khalsa College in the Punjab. He was highly influenced by the teachings of Guru Nanak and his successors as codified in the Sri Guru Granth Sahib. He came to the United States in 1913 and in July 1918 enlisted in the army. His application for American citizenship led to a controversial Supreme Court decision when it was declared "that since the 'common man's' definition of 'white' [*sic*] did not include Indians, they could not be naturalized" (History Matters 2022).

By the mid-1920s Bhagat Singh Thind started a lecture series on metaphysics that eventually took him throughout the country. Although he based much of his teachings on Sant Mat, he was eclectic in his presentations. He was fond of quoting Ralph Waldo Emerson and Walt Whitman and gave talks on health, breathing, and diet (De La Garza 2010).

His 1939 book *Radiant Road to Reality* provides an outline of his teachings, which focused on how to achieve liberation or enlightenment by Nam and Shabd bhakti. The official website devoted to his legacy summarizes it:

Nām – The Sound Within. Nām – the Holy Name is Shabda (the Word sound). Before creation, Shabda was hidden. It was Nameless. Before the Shabda, there was neither sun nor moon, nor akasha, nor fire. It was formless. "In the beginning there was the Word, the Word was with God, the Word was God." In it a desire rose and currents issued forth one after the other and through their interplay creation began. The sound-current is the most stupendous and vital fact in all the realms of nature, and to emphasize its utter importance for salvation of the soul, Saviours have come to our Humanity and bolstered this Great Truth. Every force moving from a static to a dynamic expression must vibrate from the potential to the actual, and vibration is the sound of the current running between, to, and from the universal to the individual. The great Power of the Shabda-sound current is like a magnet pulling the soul upward and without the soul's transcendence, salvation is not possible. Shabda is the spirit-sound-current, it is substance-quality-vibration, it is life-current which has originally emanated from the Supreme Being and is the only means of taking and raising the Spirit to the Source from which it emanated. Shabda is the bridge that carries the devotee across the chasm of birth and death to the bosom of the Eternal. It is like a ship carrying souls across the oceans of birth and death to the Port of Paradise in the land of Immortality. (Bhagatsinghthind 2022)

Kirpal Singh, founder of Ruhani Satsang, alleges that Bhagat Singh Thind was initiated by Sawan Singh of Radha Soami Satsang Beas and that he learned the technique of listening to the inner sound from him. "When I went to America there was one gentleman, he's passed away now, a Sikh gentleman who was giving talks on payment. His name was Dr. Bhagat Singh Thind. He married a French lady. He was initiated by Baba Sawan Singh, I know, definitely" (K. Singh 1976: 87–88).

Thind never admitted the connection and instead claimed he learned the truth from another unnamed guru. It is now well documented that Thind was familiar with Radha Soami Beas teachings, as some of his own writings were lifted (almost verbatim) from Julian P. Johnson's writings. Andrea Diem-Lane provides extensive side-by-side comparisons of the two texts in her book *The Guru in America*:

> **Radhasoami Literature:** *With a Great Master in India* (J. P. Johnson 1934; 2nd ed. 1953, 164): Gather together mind and soul, again and again, and bring them inside. Then behold a window; and beyond that an open maiden, or field. Concentrate the attention upon that and hold it there. You will see a five-colored flower garden, and inside of that, behold the Joti (candle or light). Enjoy this scene for some days. Then see the blue-colored sky appearing like a chakra (circular disc). Impelled by love and longing, pierce through this. Then gaze at the Joti with detached mind. Hear the unending bell sound and become absorbed in it. Next you will hear the conch. Let yourself become saturated with it. . . . In that region are suns and moons and stars. . . .

> **Sikh Study Group Literature:** *Radiant Road to Reality: Tested Science of Religion* (Thind 1939: 127–28): Gather together mind and soul and bring them inside. You will behold . . . a window and through its narrow passage a vast field. Steadily set your fixed gaze upon it, and keep it there until you are able to see a five-colored flower garden, and inside of it, you shall see Joti – candle or light. . . . See the blue-colored sky appearing like a circular disc; with intense longing . . . pierce through it. Keep looking and enjoying it (Joti) with detached mind. Soon you will be hearing an unending bell sound. Get yourself absorbed in it. . . . Next you will hear the conch. Let yourself become saturated with it. In this region (of Sahasdal Kanwal) are seen innumerable galaxies of suns, moons, stars. (Diem-Lane 2015: 117–18)

While the reports are basically the same, Thind replaces a few terms. For instance, he refers to the Guru as Sat-Guru and the Master's Shabd Rup as the Savior's Shabda Ray. Furthermore, Thind sometimes omits Indian references such as Johnson's mention of the "Fifth Veda." Finally, it should be noted that Thind misspells Trikuti as Tirkuti. Why? Because he is using an early edition of *With a Great Master in India* in which the typo appears. However, in later editions of Johnson's book Trikuti is correctly spelled (Diem-Lane 2015).

Dr. Bhagat Singh Thind – he earned his doctorate in the mid-1910s – wrote a number of books, including *House of Happiness* (1931) and *Science of Union with God* (1955). During his lifetime he instructed thousands in his teachings and his son, David Thind, has continued to promote his father's work and has republished a number of his books, lectures, and pamphlets. On the official Dr. Bhagat Singh Thind website, David Thind provides a hagiographical summary of his father's ministry in which he desired to continue the "transmission of truths that he gave to over five million Americans during his 56 years of teaching based on Spiritual Science or Sant Mat, the teachings of Guru Nanak, the founder of Sikhism" (Bhagatsinghthind 2022).

5. Swami Muktananda and Siddha Yoga

Swami Muktananda (1908–1982) was trained by his guru, Bhagawan Nityananda (1897–1961), in the shaktipat tradition (Muktananda 1971), where the master yogi transmits spiritual energy directly to his/her disciple, usually by touch, a sacred word, darshan, or thought transference. The belief system has much of its origin in Tantrism and has correlations with Kashmir Shaivism (Dyczkowski 1987). Although Albert Rudolph, later more widely known as Rudi or Swami Rudrananda (1928–1973), taught aspects of shaktipat (Mann 2014), it was not until Swami Muktananda made his first tour to the United States in 1970 and later established Siddha Yoga Dham Associates (SYDA) in 1976 that his distinctive shaktipat teachings became widely known (Prakashananda 2007).

Muktananda's autobiography, *The Play of Consciousness* (1971), is revealing about his years practicing spiritual sadhana and what he achieved through arduous hours of yoga and meditation. Besides having ecstatic visions, culminating in his beholding the "blue pearl," which he claims makes one "the most blessed of all human beings," Muktananda describes at length hearing inner sounds, which he refers to as nada.

> In the meditation which follows Kundalini awakening, the inner music, or nada, of So'ham can be heard, and all a seeker needs to do is keep listening to it all the time. Nothing is higher than this nada. Once you begin to hear it in the spiritual center at the crown of the head you will hear it vibrating every particle of your body. This is the voice of God (Siddhayoga.org 2022a).

Listening to the inner sound current has become a key element in all of SYDA's teachings. After Muktananda's death there was a succession dispute between Swami Chidvilasananda and her brother, Swami Nityananda, which led to a split that has never been mended. Today Swami Chidvilasananda – known among her followers as Gurumayi – is the sole head of Muktananda's organization (L. Harris

1994). She has a large following despite the fallout that occurred, and that continues, after *The CoEvolution Quarterly* (Winter 1983) published Willam Rodarmor's "The Secret Life of Swami Mutkananda," which graphically detailed the guru's many sexual transgressions and fondness for money (Forman & Fishelman 2014).

Today the SYDA has many centers around the world, with a large presence in India, Australia, and the United States. Gurumayi states that her mission is for "awakening seekers to their own potential for enlightenment," which is accomplished by "bestowing shaktipat" (Shaktipat Intensive n.d.). Siddha yoga's emphasis on nada yoga has similarities with the Divine Light Mission, since both groups have developed breathing techniques found in the *Gheranda Samhita*, where the inhaling and exhaling of one's breath follows the sound of "So'ham."

On the official SYDA website are several testimonies given by Siddha Yoga students about the efficacy of hearing the sound current:

> I began to coordinate my in-breath and out-breath with the mantra So'ham in meditation. I experienced that each breath was radiating tiny particles of scintillating light, all vibrating with the primordial sound of AUM. It seemed to me that my whole being consisted of these tiny shimmering particles of light, vibrating in unison.
>
> Last February, when I arrived for the Pilgrimage to the Heart Retreat in Gurudev Siddha Peeth, I felt Baba's grace descend upon me, and I experienced the ongoing inner nada expanding out, encompassing the sacred grounds of the Ashram. As I walked along the garden paths, the divine nada seemed to permeate all the trees and plants, and I could see sparkling particles dancing in the air. Time stopped, perception of separation disappeared, and all that existed was the bliss of nada (Siddhayoga.org 2022a).

Paul Twitchell and Eckankar

Eckankar was founded by Paul Twitchell (1909–1971) in California in the mid-1960s. Although the Hindi/Punjabi term *Ek Onkar* (literally "One God/Power") was most likely derived from Guru Nanak's *Japji* (the first set of hymns in the Sikh holy book, Sri Guru Granth Sahib), Twitchell altered its original phonetic spelling and definition, claiming that Eckankar was a Tibetan-Pali word meaning "coworker with God." According to Twitchell, Eckankar was an ancient spiritual path with a lineage of 970 "Eck" Masters who trace back to Gakko, who brought the true teachings of soul travel from the city of Retz on the planet Venus. Twitchell alleged that through this bilocation philosophy a neophtye can leave his or her body via an inner light and sound and soul-travel to higher regions of consciousness, which lead ultimately to the supreme lord, Sugmad.

The Living Eck Master, occasionally retaining the more exalted title of Mahanta, the highest state of God consciousness on earth, is central to Eckankar theology because it is through his guidance that the student, known as a chela, receives various levels of initiation, usually involving instructions into new sacred tones and other higher-level practices of contemplation. In an early article entitled "The Cliff Hanger" Twitchell explained the basis behind his new group: "Eckankar, which I formed out of my own experience, is the term used for the philosophy I have developed for the Cliff Hanger. It is based on Shabd-Yoga, a way out form of yoga. The word is the Hindu locution for the cosmic sound current which is known in our vernacular as the cosmic river of God" (Lane 1983; Lane 2020a: 41).

Eckankar has weathered a fair storm of controversy since its inception, primarily because of questions concerning Twitchell's alleged plagiarism, biographical redactions, and purported historical antecedents. First, Twitchell claimed that while traveling in Europe and India he was taught Eckankar by the two former Masters who preceded him, Sudar Singh of Allahabad and Rebazar Tarzs, a supposed five-hundred-year-old Tibetan monk. However, there is no documented evidence proving that Twitchell visited these countries when he claimed he did or that either Sudar Singh or Rebazar Tarzs are genuine historical figures. Rather, there is ample evidence – even from Twitchell's own pen – that he was associated with Swami Premananda of the Self-Revelation Church of Absolute Monism in Washington, DC, from 1950 to 1955, when he was asked to leave the church for personal misconduct. Additionally, Twitchell received initiation into shabd yoga in 1955 from Kirpal Singh, the founder of Ruhani Satsang in Delhi, India, while the guru was on his first tour of the United States. He kept in close contact with Kirpal Singh via correspondence for at least a decade and took his wife, Gail, to see the Indian guru and have her receive initiation from him in San Francisco in 1963. Twitchell also joined L. Ron Hubbard's Church of Scientology in the 1950s and eventually served for a short time as his press agent and wrote a number of articles for the group. With the founding of Eckankar, however, Twitchell altered his biography and redacted references to his former teachers and replaced them with a hierarchy of Eck Masters. A number of Twitchell's books on Eckankar contain large chunks of material appropriated from sources he failed to reference. Twitchell seemed particularly fond of plagiarizing whole passages from Radha Soami Satsang Beas author Julian Johnson, whose two books, *With a Great Master in India* (1934) and *The Path of the Masters* (1939), contributed to much of Eckankar's specialized terminology that draws extensively from the Sant Mat tradition of North India, an eclectic spiritual movement that includes such poet-saints as Kabir, Dadu, and Tulsi Sahib (F. Johnson 2003; Marman 2007).

As the former president of Eckankar, Dr. Louis Bluth, confessed in a letter dated June 19, 1980, after Paul Twitchell's death:

> My wife and I opened the first Eck class in Sun City, Cal. I personally treated Paul [Twitchell] many times and was the main speaker in Cincinnati when he passed away. Paul was a sincere student in the beginning and I considered him honest. Problems between him and his wife Gail led him to believe she was going to leave him and he desperately wanted to keep her. So when she demanded more money and better living, he started to write things and copy from other books. [Paul Twitchell] borrowed my books on Radha Soami and copied a large share from them. I helped him write the Herb book and went to Riverside University and took Sanskrit, so basically much of the material is good because it is copied. I confronted him with what he had done and his answer was "since the author of the book said it better than I could I copied it." The trouble is that he never gave anyone credit as to where he got it.
>
> (Lane 2020a: 174–75)

Eckankar has become an exceptionally successful religion with centers spanning the globe. Interestingly, Eckankar has a strong presence in Africa, particularly Nigeria, and in Europe, and it continues to draw thousands to its yearly conferences. Eckankar has been directly influenced by the SRF, Theosophy, Scientology, and particularly Sant Mat via its specialized version of sound-current yoga. It has in turn influenced a number of new religious offshoots, including the Movement of Spiritual Inner Awareness (MSIA) founded by John-Roger Hinkins, MasterPath founded by Gary Olsen, the Ancient Teachings of the Masters (ATOM) founded by Darwin Gross, the Divine Science of Light and Sound founded by Jerry Mulvin, the Sonic Spectrum founded by Michael Turner, and the Higher Consciousness Society founded by Ford Johnson. Each of the founders of these groups was at one time a member of Eckankar, and they have all incorporated many Eck terms and ideas into their respective organizations. Eckankar's future looks bright as it enters its fifth decade of existence.

While Twitchell made the sound current, or Eck, a cardinal feature of his teachings, he argued that his understanding and practice of it was unique, since he came from an unbroken lineage of masters that was distinct from Radhasoami. In the *Shariyat-ki-Sugmad* (1971), one of the holy scriptures of Eckankar, Twitchell describes the shabd thusly:

> The Word, the Voice of the Sugmad [God], goes forth like a wave from the center of a pond and sings Its way through all the planes in many different songs and melodies. Each is the living Word, creating and giving life to everything in each world. By Its very life – this ECK, the essence of the Sugmad, the Spirit of all things – life exists. When It reaches the end of the

worlds It returns like the wave, gathering up all Souls that are ready to do God's work. They are returned to the true home and become Co-workers with God, having completed their mission in life. (Twitchell 1971b: 68)

The current leader of Eckankar is Harold Klemp (b. 1942), who succeeded Darwin Gross, who was previously appointed by Twitchell's widow, Gail Atkinson, after her husband died in 1971 (Albrecht & Alexander 1979). Klemp, who excommunicated his predecessor after a contentious legal battle, has spread the Eckankar teachings throughout the world, gathering a significant following in Africa. He has published a number of books, including *Spiritual Exercises of Eck* (1993), *The Art of Spiritual Dreaming* (1999), and *Autobiography of a Modern Prophet* (2000). After Darwin Gross was excommunicated from Eckankar, all of his books were removed from sale. His picture and even a detailed description of his tenure has been excised from all of Eckankar's related materials.

Eckankar members use the Hu chant as one of their key mantras and in meetings with their spiritual leader, Harold Klemp. The mantra often begins with those in attendance, usually several thousand, chanting the word in a melodious fashion. Eckankar's official website explains:

> HU is an ancient name for God. It has been used for thousands of years as a prayer and sacred chant to attune oneself to the presence of God. Millions of people around the world have experienced the joy of HU. In many spiritual traditions, sound plays an important part in uplifting the individual. HU is a key to open your heart to God's loving presence in your life. Anyone can sing HU, regardless of age or religion. It is a simple technique that can be used as part of your daily spiritual practice. It has the power to uplift you spiritually for inner peace, healing, and insight. It is a gift to you, and for anyone looking to experience more divine love in life.
>
> (Eckankar.org 2022)

It is evident that Klemp and Twitchell's invocation of the Hu is based primarily on Sufism (Khan 1996). Eckankar's promotion of the sound current as central to its teachings can be gleaned from many of Twitchell's books and articles. One significant change Twitchell brought about in Eckankar was his restructuring of the traditional Radhasoami/Ruhani Satsang eight-plane cosmology. Twitchell did this, though, only after having used the original Sant Mat cosmology in several of his earlier books – most notably in *The Tiger's Fang* (1967) and *The Far Country* (1971a). The intriguing aspect is that Twitchell's revised and copyrighted twelve-plane cosmology, which is given in the Spiritual Notebook and was standard in Eckankar by 1971, contravenes his previous eight-plane one. The following is a comparison chart of the two cosmologies that we developed (Lane 1983).

Original (based upon the Sant and Radhasoami traditions; depicted in Twitchell's earliest books on Eckankar):

1. Sahasra dal Kanwal: sounds – bell and conch
2. Brahm Lok (Trikuti): sounds – big drum (thunder)
3. Daswan Dwar: sounds – violins (sarangi)
4. Bhanwar Gupha: sounds – flute
5. Sach Khand: sounds – vina (bagpipe)
6. Alakh Lok – nameless
7. Agam Lok – nameless
8. Anami Lok (Sugmad) – nameless

Revised (as given in the *Spiritual Notebook* and standard by 1971):

1. Elam (Physical): sounds – thunder
2. Sat Kanwal Anda (Astral): sounds – roar of the sea
3. Maha–Kal/Par Brahm (Causal): sounds – tinkle of bells
4. Brahmanda Brahm (Mental): sounds – running water
5. Sat Nam (Soul): sounds – single note of flute
6. Alakh Lok: sounds – heavy wind
7. Alaya Lok: sounds – deep humming
8. Hukikat Lok: sounds – a thousand violins
9. Agam Lok: sounds – music of woodwinds
10. Anami Lok: sounds – whirlpool
11. Sugmad Lok: sounds – music of universe
12. Sugmad/Living Reality: sounds – music of God

The most noticeable difference in the two cosmologies is in the location of the various sounds, known in Radhasoami as shabd dhuns. Note that in the first eight-plane cosmology the sound of the flute is heard on the fourth plane, Bhanwar gupha, one region below Sach Khand, the eternal soul realm, whereas in the twelve-plane chart the sound of the flute is heard on the fifth plane, Sat Nam, the soul region. This difference, while perhaps not noteworthy in any other spiritual tradition, is elemental in shabd yoga, where the whole essence of the path is based upon the internal hearing of the sound current or audible life stream. The knowledge of which sounds to listen to and which to discard is an extremely important part of the teachings. Other variances in the cosmologies include: (1) The sound of the thunder that was heard in Trikuti, the causal realm, in the original Sant Mat cosmology is now, according to the twelve-plane chart, heard in the physical region, Elam. (2) The tinkle of bells that was originally heard up to and through the first plane, Sahasra dal Kanwal, is now heard in the third region, MahaKal-Par-Brahm. (3) Par Brahm, which used to be in Daswan Dwar – beyond mind and matter – is now in the causal realm, a region that was previously in Trikuti, the home of the mind. The preceding comparisons are important in understanding that, although Twitchell employed basic Sant Mat concepts in the beginning of his group, the teachings themselves have undergone an evolution in Eckankar. This not only signals Twitchell breaking off from Ruhani Satsang doctrines via his former guru, Kirpal Singh, but it also indicates an evolving and not stationary superstructure within Eckankar. More precisely, what may have been taught in Eckankar in 1965 and 1966 may not necessarily be disseminated today (Lane 1983; F. Johnson 2003; Marman 2007).

Eckankar is not unique in altering its sound current cosmology, since the same has occurred to varying degrees in other yogic movements as well. It is of interest to note which sound is considered the highest or the last in various yoga manuals and traditions. Sometimes it is thunder or a drum, sometimes it is the flute, and sometimes it is the vina. Invariably, though, the texts speak of that sound that is ultimately "soundless." What is intriguing here, from both a sociological and a historical perspective, is to chart the evolution of certain core ideas and techniques and how they can remain relatively the same over the course of time and/or be modified depending on the circumstance.

After the ascension of Harold Klemp a number of offshoots of Eckankar have developed that share much of its theology but that in turn have developed their own unique variations.

1. John-Roger Hinkins and the Movement of Spiritual Inner Awareness (MSIA)

In 1968 John-Roger Hinkins (1934–2014), who was raised in the Church of Latter-day Saints and became a high school teacher, started his spiritual ministry in Rosemead, California. He named it the Movement of Spiritual Inner Awareness (MSIA). John-Roger, or JR as he was affectionately termed, was associated with Paul Twitchell and Eckankar, having been a mail correspondence member and a second initiate. There are also reports that he was connected with other metaphysical groups, learning firsthand about meditation, light attunement, and aura balancing, which he later incorporated into his own movement (Lewis 1998; McWilliams 1994).

Although John-Roger's name appears in Twitchell's newsletter, dated in the late 1960s, as a convener for Eckankar-sponsored meetings in Southern California, John-Roger did not view his connection with Paul Twitchell as a master/disciple or teacher/student relationship. The fact remains, however, that his group and his teachings are almost exactly the same as those taught by Paul Twitchell, not even excepting particular Twitchellian nuances. Likewise, some MSIA initiates recall that in the early meetings JR would "call in" the spirit of brother Paul Twitchell as a master conversant in soul travel (Lane 1984).

The MSIA's organizational structure is almost parallel to that of Twitchell's group with regard to initiation, discourses, and cosmology. John-Roger is known to members of the MSIA as the physical manifestation of the Mystical Traveler Consciousness (MTC), an all-powerful inner spirit that guides the progress of soul travelers. This concept, by the way, is quite similar to the Satguru in the Radhasoami tradition and the Mahanta in Eckankar. According to Hinkins's account, the mantle of the MTC passed to him in or around 1963. During this time he claims to have met Sawan Singh, the late Radha Soami Satsang Beas master who died in 1948. He holds that Sawan Singh was the previous receptor of the MTC and passed on the keys to the kingdom to him on the inner spiritual planes. In the beginning, however, JR did not recognize the luminous being as Sawan Singh. At first, he alleged to be in communication with Rebazar Tarzs, a five-hundred-year-old Tibetan monk, who was a fictional character Paul Twitchell created to hide his past associations. Accordingly, it was only later when Roger saw a photograph of the Radhasoami guru that he placed the picture of Sawan Singh with the powerful entity he encountered in meditation. Before Hinkins died he appointed John Morton as his successor. While the MSIA acknowledges that it looks similar to other religions, it argues that it is unique:

> MSIA has been described as being similar or connected with various groups, i.e., Sant Mat, Christian Charismatics, Radha Soami, Eckankar, Science of Mind, and many other religious groups. In fact, however, MSIA is a new look at ancient teachings – teachings that may parallel many that are taught in other faiths. MSIA has something for everyone, which is perhaps why people have associated it with so many other religions. What makes MSIA unique is the Mystical Traveler Consciousness, which works directly with students in MSIA. (MSIA.org 2022)

Since the inception of the MSIA, John-Roger has infused his group with a variety of teachings, practices, and New Age techniques from other spiritual traditions. The central tenet focuses on the sound current and the MTC. For instance, compare the MSIA's cosmology, as found in *The Sound Current* (Hinkins 1976), with Twitchell's cosmology, as found in *The Spiritual Notebook* (Twitchell 1971c).

Paul Twitchell's Cosmology (Region and Sound)

1. Physical (Thunder)
2. Astral (Roar of the Sea)
3. Causal (Tinkle of Bells)
4. Mental (Running Water)
5. Soul (Single Note of Flute)
6. Alakh Lok (Heavy Wind)
7. Alaya Lok (Deep Humming)
8. Hukikat Lok (One Thousand Violins)
9. Agam Lok (Music of Woodwinds)

John-Roger Hinkins's Cosmology (Region and Sound)

1. Physical (Thunder)
2. Astral (Roaring Surf)
3. Causal (Tinkle of Bells)
4. Mental (Running Water)
5. Soul (Sound of Flute)

[After the fifth level Hinkins doesn't number the next sounds.]

Sound of Wind
Humming Sound
Ten Thousand Violins
Sound of Woodwinds

John-Roger's cosmology is exactly the same as Paul Twitchell's. This is unusual because of Twitchell's own creative implantations, which were uniquely his own. Both of these schemas represent a distinct departure from the Radhasoami esoteric version, which was the primary source for Twitchell's understanding of the sound current and surat shabd yoga practice.

John-Roger would often incorporate terminology from other shabd yoga-related movements and then redefine them in light of his own teachings. A good illustration of this is how he introduced *Sarmad* as a term for God, apparently changing it from the Eckankar word *Sugmad*. John-Roger transposed Twitchell's term *Sugmad*, which stands for the Highest Lord, into the MSIA's *Sarmad*. In any case, Sarmad is actually the name given for a famous Jewish-Sufi mystic of the seventeenth century in India who died a martyr because of his claim that he was one with God (Asiri 2021).

Coincidentally, John-Roger has also taken over the five-name mantra from the Radha Soami Satsang Beas and Ruhani Satsangs. In doing so, though, he has rearranged the order in two of the names, showing once again how he has adopted earlier terminology and altered it for his own purposes. In several personal interviews with John-Roger, both face-to-face and on the phone (1977 to 1983), he once quite candidly told us the five "sacred tones" that he gave out sequentially to his students. These were identical to the five-name mantra given out at initiation at Radha Soami Satsang Beas and most of these groups related to them (such as Kirpal Singh's Ruhani Satsang). Apparently Hinkins learned them directly from a former disciple of Charan Singh. However, he juxtaposed the second name with the third, reversing the order.

John-Roger Hinkins and the MSIA advocate listening to the inner sound current and suggest that it is a direct method for attaining God-Realization:

> There is a Sound of God on each level, otherwise known as the Sound Current. The Sound is a very high form of ultimate reality. Once you get into the Soul realm and above, the Light is not seen in exactly the same way as it is in the lower realms. It is impressed on you and heard. It is primarily Sound and secondly Light. Accordingly, on every level of Light, in every plane, in every dimension, there is a keeper of the Sound Current. Appointed by Sat Nam, this is the one who is granted the keys to the Sound Current and who is known as the Mystical Traveler Consciousness. The Traveler has the keys on every realm for the flow of Light and the Sound Current. The Sound Current does not necessarily work by your calling on it. With the Sound Current, you have to move your consciousness into it. (MSIA.org 2022)

What is most intriguing is how John-Roger redefines which sounds the aspirant should hear and on which level of consciousness. Where the Sant and Radhasoami traditions relegate the buzzing sound to the first plane, Hinkins locates it higher up on the etheric plane. He also lists a much larger database of sounds, claiming that there are "at least 27 levels above Soul with concomitant sounds." He elaborates:

> On the astral level, the Sound Current is akin to the whoosh of ocean surf. On the causal, it's chimes, or tinkling bells, a very delicate sound. In the mental level, it's like running water or a tumbling brook. In the etheric, it's a buzzing sound, such as made by a bee or a fly.
>
> In the Soul, there is a flute-like sound, but it is not an ordinary flute. It is a haunting, almost drawing-to-you sound. It's not tugging because you'll have no resistance. You will go to it. That is the sound referred to in the Bible: In the beginning was the Word, and the Word was with God, and the Word was God. That is a sound from the Soul level of God, which exists perennially in each person. To hear only takes awakening to that which comes through the Soul. There are at least 27 levels above Soul with concomitant sounds. When you get above the first level, the sound is like a cool summer wind blowing through easily swaying trees. (MSIA.org 2022)

Hinkins also connects with both Sufism and Eckankar in mentioning the efficacy of the Hu sound and how it is heard when one transcends the third level of soul. He is much more descriptive in detailing the ins and outs of which sounds one may hear.

> Above that level, it sounds as if thousands of violins are playing or angels are singing. It is the beautiful sound that is often described in Greek mythology. The allegories of the Sound of God and the sound that comes from the heavens exist in literature throughout recorded time. When Jesus said that the wind comes where it comes and goes where it goes and that no one knows where it comes and where it goes, he was referring to the Sound of God. (John 3:8) When you get above the third level of Soul, into the inaccessible levels, you hear the sound of HU. Just the HU described in words or reproduced with the HU-man voice. They are inner sounds beyond description on the physical level. (MSIA.org 2022)

The MSIA offers soul transcendence and various level of initiations where the student receives different tones or names for their spiritual growth. In 1988 John-Roger Hinkins passed "the keys to the Mystical Traveler Consciousness to John Morton" and they worked together as spiritual guides until he died in 2014 (MSIA.org 2022).

2. Gary Olsen and MasterPath

Gary Olsen (b. 1948) was a follower of Eckankar for several years, but he branched off and started his own group, MasterPath, after Harold Klemp took over from Darwin Gross. MasterPath teachings draw primarily from two sources: Eckankar and Radha Soami Satsang Beas (Holtje 1995; Diem-Lane 2015). However, Gary Olsen believes that his movement stands out from the rest, even if there are striking similarities.

1. The presence of a true Guru, in contrast to a pseudo guru: A "Sat," or true, Guru is commissioned by the Highest, while pseudo gurus are self-commissioned. A true Guru is sanctioned to initiate the soul into the spiritual Current, while pseudo gurus desire the devotee to worship the personality of the guru, or even one's own personality.
2. The pursuit of the Sound Current, in contradistinction to the light: The Sound is the primordial Current emanating from the Supreme Deity, while the light is the vast array of mental knowledge issuing forth from the mental realms.
3. Attainment of Self and God Realization before the translation of the physical body: Spiritual liberation is the goal. (MasterPath.org)

Unlike Paul Twitchell and John-Roger Hinkins, Gary Olsen claims he was Swateh Saint, born as an enlightened master, and that he has a direct connection with Anami, or the highest state of being. He does not mention any intermediaries, such as Rebazar Tarzs or Sawan Singh, passing on their mantle to him. The idea of a born saint is not unique to MasterPath, as similar claims have been made about Kabir, Guru Nanak, Tulsi Sahib, and Shiv Dayal Singh. Arguably, by not connecting to a previous lineage, the new master can be free from any succession disputes that may arise from rivals. Genealogical dissociation is a much more common occurrence in new religious movements, and in old ones as well, than one might at first suspect. This is not surprising since claiming to be sui generis offers the would-be guru and his organization much more latitude than being bound to the earlier traditions to which he or she is beholden. In response to a query posted on Olsen's website about the necessity of getting initiation from a competent master, even if one becomes a master himself or herself, he gave the following exception:

> You are exactly right. Although receiving the spiritual mantle through credible lineage is the accepted way in ninety-nine percent of the cases, it is not the only way. Founding saints who descend from the heights of anami lok do not technically require the outer initiation, for they descended directly from the godhead and are already divinely ignited and appointed through anami's perfect love and mercy. This was the case with both Guru Nanak and with Swami Ji of Agra, for they were also responsible for founding new lineages of living Masters. However, even the param saints must refamiliarize themselves with the light and sound doctrine when they enter a new incarnation. Thus, since the earmark of a param saint's arrival is the customary absence of a fully realized Master, in their great humility these founding saints take initiation from a lesser order of Master, or in some cases even a self-realized soul, and they serve and fulfill all of the requirements of true chelaship.
>
> (Olsen 2005: 121)

Olsen goes on to admit, however, that he was exposed to shabd yoga teachings when he saw Charan Singh in Minneapolis, Minnesota, on his first world tour in 1964 and that years later he took initiation from Darwin Gross of Eckankar, with whom he associated for more than a decade (Olsen 2005).

In an effort to separate himself from both traditions, Gary Olsen explained that:

> But in truth, none of these wonderful Teachings can be given the exclusive credit for my own initiation, liberation, and ensuing salvation, for Anami Purush is my true Lord and Master, nor is the MasterPath an extension of any of these aforementioned paths, for it was Anami Purush who graciously sanctioned, commissioned, and orchestrated the inception of Masterpath and its current living Master in July of 1987. (Olsen 2005: 121)

Yet, in publishing his many books on MasterPath, Olsen, like Paul Twitchell of Eckankar, appropriated large parts of Radha Soami Satsang Beas publications without attribution. Such accusations of plagiarism led Olsen to issue a worldwide apology on the Internet in 1995, wherein he wrote:

> MasterPath has utilized a number of Radhasoami Satsang Beas publications in their written discourses. However, it has not properly cited or referenced these copyrighted materials. MasterPath regrets this mistake and is committed to revising all of their publications in order to clearly identify Radhasoami masters and books when quoted. MasterPath accepts full responsibility for improperly using copyrighted materials and will refrain from doing so in the future. MasterPath also apologizes for any confusion this may have caused.
>
> (Lane & Diem-Lane 2020: 2)

Andrea Diem-Lane has provided extensive documentation of MasterPath's appropriations from Radhasoami books, particularly Charan Singh's *Word Eternal*. Here are three key side-by-side comparisons of the hundred or more that have been found.

> Charan Singh, *Words Eternal*: The doctrine of karma is not against making any effort but teaches us to be content when our efforts fail (43).
>
> Gary Olsen, *MasterPath Book II*: The doctrine of karma is not against making any effort but teaches us to be content when our efforts seemingly fail (97).
>
> Charan Singh, *Words Eternal*: To lose our own identity and to become another being is love. ... Who are the true devotees of the Lord? Not those who know the most, but those who love the most (96–98).
>
> Gary Olsen, *MasterPath Book II*: To lose our own identity and to become another being is love. ... Who are the true devotees of the Master? Not those who know the most, but those who love the most (99).
>
> Charan Singh, *Words Eternal*: Without Divine Grace Satguru cannot be contacted. Without Satguru Nam cannot be obtained. Without Nam there can be no salvation. Such is the essence of the Path of the Masters. ... In this world we accept a reflection for real, a counterfeit for genuine, a piece of glass for a diamond (99–100).
>
> Gary Olsen, *MasterPath Book II*: Without Divine Grace, the Sat Guru cannot be contacted. Without the Sat Guru, Shabda cannot be obtained. Without Shabda, there can be no liberation. ... Such is the essence of the MasterPath. ... In this world we accept a reflection for real, a counterfeit for genuine, and a piece of glass for a diamond (99).
>
> (Diem-Lane 2015: 73–76)

It appears that the key source material here for Gary Olsen are three Radha Soami Satsang Beas books – *Discourses on Sant Mat* by Sawan Singh, *The Path of the Masters* by Julian P. Johnson, and *Science of the Soul* by Jagat Singh. Each contains extensive glossaries. Olsen used these books as part of the glossary material in his third volume of *MasterPath: The Divine Science of Light and Sound*. In the letter of acknowledgment to his book (published in May 1999; two thousand copies), Olsen claims that MasterPath teachings mostly parallel the writings of Sawan Singh and other saints within the Sant Mat tradition. However, he neglects to mention that his book also copies, sometimes verbatim, from that same literature without direct references or quotes. The interested reader should keep in mind that the Radha Soami Beas literature MasterPath appropriates was published and copyrighted at least three decades before Olsen's book. Ironically, Gary Olsen also copyrights his own works, even the ones with extensive plagiarism, with the declaration of "all rights reserved" (J. P. Johnson 1939; J. Singh 1959; S. Singh 1963; Olsen 1999).

When Gary Olsen branched off to start his own movement, he systematically began to incorporate the writings of earlier Radhasoami gurus. His initial plagiarism in the early 1990s was much more blatant. For example, in one case he didn't even bother to create his own cosmological map but instead simply photocopied a chakra illustration directly from the Radha Soami Beas publication *Call of the Great Master* by Daryai Lal Kapur and whited out the page citation (J. P. Johnson 1939; J. Singh 1959; S. Singh 1963; Olsen 1999).

What is intriguing from a sociological and historical perspective is to see the minor changes that Olsen makes to the original text from which he copies his material. In our first sample, for instance, he changes "when our efforts fail" to "when our efforts *seemingly* fail." In sample two Olsen replaces "true devotees of the Lord" with "true devotees of the Master." In sample three he replaces "Nam" with "Shabda" and "Path of the Masters" with "MasterPath." These changes, though minor, demonstrate how certain ideas can be modified over time in ways that may at first may not be noticed but that may loom more significantly later on, as we have concerning which sounds one is supposed to hear during meditation.

Olsen uses the word "contemplation" instead of "meditation" and suggests that students listening to the sound current do so only twenty to thirty minutes a day, arguing that Radhasoami's insistence on two and half hours is too demanding and leads to disappointment when such a time allotment is not fulfilled. In this regard, Olsen is following Eckankar's lead, which also uses the term *contemplation* and suggests less than a half an hour for spiritual exercises. Today MasterPath has attracted several thousand followers and keeps a relatively low profile, with Gary Olsen only offering seminars to his initiates three to four times a year along with maintaining a website with a special section for initiates only.

3. Darwin Gross and the Ancient Teachings of the Masters (ATOM)

When Darwin Gross (1928–2008) appointed Harold Klemp as the Living Eck Master in 1981, he had no idea that two years later his successor would excommunicate him from Eckankar, ban his books from sale, and instigate a lawsuit against him for business impropriety and copyright infringement. But that is exactly what happened. In a "Personal and Confidential" letter dated January 4, 1984, Harold Klemp informed Darwin Gross of his removal from Eckankar:

> The Order of the Vairagi ECK Masters no longer recognizes you as an ECK Master. As the agent of the ECK, I have removed all of your initiations in ECK as well as terminated your membership in ECKANKAR. You are not capable or authorized to act or speak for or about the Vairagi ECK Masters, ECKANKAR or the ECK teachings, nor are you to hold yourself out as an ECK Master or ECK member. Do not directly or indirectly associate yourself or your activities with the sacred teachings of ECK or ECKANKAR in any way. I have refrained from coming forth with this pronouncement sooner for the sake of those new to the path and still setting their spiritual foundation. Dap Ren [the spiritual name for Darwin Gross] served the ECK well at one time but the negative forces were allowed in through lack of vigilance and discipline, causing spiritual decay. No one has done this to you – you have brought this upon yourself. (Lane 1983: 103)

Naturally, Darwin Gross did not accept Klemp's excommunication, since it was Gross himself who appointed Klemp as the Living Eck Master. In a letter dated February 1984 and widely distributed among interested Eck chelas, Gross presented his own version of the breach between Klemp and himself: "Many individuals who are spiritually awake are concerned about the misguided information coming out of Menlo Park. The Vairagi Masters do recognize me as a Vairagi Master. My initiations cannot be removed by Harold or anyone else. Harold Klemp does not have that authority. He was given a spiritual responsibility, which he has lost. He no longer holds the Rod of Eck Power" (Lane 2020a: 104).

Darwin Gross explained further that:

> ECKANKAR has initiated legal action against me, dated August 20, 1983, and I was forced to go out and find a lawyer in Portland. This is not the way of honorable and ethical human beings. People have been listening to misguided Higher Initiates who have been told by Menlo Park to remove my pictures, destroy my writings, tapes and music, and this has not been authorized by me; it is under the control and guise of someone working in the psychic world. Neither Paul Twitchell nor I have planned any of this psychic negativism that has been coming out (of) Menlo Park. It smacks of control and fear. What has

been happening is taking away the individual's freedom of choice. Those individuals who have been reporting psychic attacks and concern about magicians need to ask Divine Spirit or SUGMAD, where is the spiritual protection that Eckist has? Have they been receiving spiritual protection from Harold Klemp? It does not appear so. (Lane 2020a: 104–5)

Darwin Gross did not prevail in the legal suits that were filed and so he established his own movement, which he eventually named with the acronym ATOM, Ancient Teachings of the Masters. He continued to teach the same Eck concepts, though he was forced to use different vocabulary to express them since Eckankar protected its trademark terms from infringement.

Gross's group never became successful, attracting only a few hundred followers during his lifetime. He nevertheless offered a hierarchy of initiations, which followed the standard God-Worlds chart Twitchell had developed in *The Spiritual Notebook* (1971). Pierre Zoccatelli elaborates on Gross's belief system:

> After two years of study, the student may receive the Light and Sound Initiation, through which he/she may become part of the cosmic Sound Current. After five years or more, he/she becomes eligible to receive the Soul Initiation. The course of the initiation follows the "God Worlds Chart," composed of thirteen levels, with a sound corresponding to each. For example, corresponding to the physical, astral, causal, mental, and ethereal levels are, respectively, thunder, the ocean's roar, the sound of bells, the flow of water, and the buzzing of bees, and the sound-words Alay, Kala, Aum, Mana, and Baju. When the individual has passed through the "Tunnel of Yreka," and has entered the "Soul Plane," he/she is free to move on his/her own. Beyond this world are invisible worlds, endless worlds, a God consciousness plane, the inaccessible, the nameless, the Sugmad Lok and lastly the world of Sugmad. At these levels, starting from that of the soul, correspond the sounds and melodies of a single note of the flute, a strong wind, a deep singing with closed mouth, thousands of violins, music for wind instruments, the sound of a vortex, music of the universe, and music of God. The corresponding sound-words are Sugma, Shanti, Hum, Aluk, Huk, Hu and, lastly, the Unspoken Word. (Zoccatelli 2006: 32–33)

What Gross and other leaders of new religious movements focusing on shabd yoga have done is slightly alter the sounds one hears in deep contemplation, making distinctive nuances that make them stand apart from their predecessors. This can range from introducing a new melody, such as "the sound of a vortex," to a slight spelling alteration as we saw with John-Roger Hinkins's "Sarmad."

Darwin Gross's following continued to dwindle after he left Eckankar and his organization, the ATOM, never achieved mainstream success. At public meetings, which were infrequent, around fifty initiates and seekers would attend. As Dodie Bellamy, a former Eckist, explains:

> Gross continues to work as a spiritual master, with a small group of devoted followers, many of them former Eckists. He publishes books through an organization called *Be Good to Your Self*, located in Las Vegas. Home study discourses and musical tapes are also available. Much of Gross's current teachings center around the easy-listening jazz he performs on the vibes. Gross's uplifting music is claimed to have miraculous healing powers. ... We take our seats among the 50 or so other seekers, many of whom have flown in for the event. Dawn is finishing an applied kinesiology demonstration of the power of Gross's music. A volunteer raises one arm straight out to the side, and Dawn easily pushes it down. Then she asks him to think about Gross's music as he again holds out his arm. This time the arm doesn't budge no matter how hard she pushes down on it. "See!" she exclaims. We close our eyes and chant Hu together for several minutes. Gross enters and takes his position behind the gold-toned vibes.
>
> (Bellamy 1995)

Since Darwin Gross's death in 2008, what remains of his organization is a simple website without much information (atom.org). However, Eckankar has continued to grow worldwide and has become one of the most visible new religious movements to have emerged out of the 1960s.

4. Jerry Mulvin and Internet Gurus

Darwin Gross's departure led to an exodus of a number of Eckankar members, several of whom, like Gary Olsen, started their own ministries. One of the first was Jerry Mulvin, who set up his organization in Manhattan Beach, California, but later moved his operation to Scottsdale, Arizona. He published three books that advertised his new path, the Divine Science of Light and Sound. Following closely the teaching of Eckankar, Mulvin explains in his first book, *The Annals of Time*:

> In November 1979 I received physical verification of Mastership; my final initiation that had already taken place in the formless worlds. At long last – a meeting on the Physical Plane with my Guardian Angel. There he sat in plain view, Fubbi Quantz. His eyes gleamed like mirrors and reflected me. My only thoughts were, "I'm looking into the eyes of the Master." ... From that moment on, the "Great Ones," Fubbi Quantz and Rebazar Tarz, have been the guiding force behind me. (Diem-Lane 2015: 67)

Like his predecessors, Mulvin taught that listening to the sound current was the highest pathway to achieve enlightenment. He consciously connected with the previous Eckankar masters, but put a new spin on how and why the mastership had passed on to him. Instead of offering a series of initiations,

Mulvin provided what he calls a "connection." This is secured for a yearly membership fee of one hundred dollars.

Jerry Mulvin's spiritual career, however, was seriously derailed when he was arrested in May 1998 for having child pornography on his computer. He has kept a low profile ever since.

Eckankar, MasterPath, the ATOM, and the Divine Science of Light and Sound all request a financial payment for joining their respective groups. This differentiates them from most of the shabd yoga groups in India, which have no such monetary stipulations. However, the Radhasoami groups do accept donations and this has generated tremendous income over the years.

With the advent of the World Wide Web, developed by Tim Berners-Lee, a new religious phenomenon occurred: the rise of Internet gurus. These were individuals who had no formal organization or any significant following but who went online and started their own ministries from scratch. A number of these Internet gurus preached a version of shabd yoga. Included in this diversified assemblage are the late Michael Martin, Michael Turner, Sri Allen Feldman, Christopher Tims, Duane Hepner, and many others. While most of these individuals have not garnered much attention or many followers, they do represent how new technologies can open hitherto unknown markets. Essentially, anyone with a Net presence – from a website to a Facebook account to a YouTube channel – can become a focal point to share their teachings. The ability to create one's own self-styled religious movement is remarkably easy today, though there is no assurance that it will be successful in garnering a significant following. Even whimsical groups, which at first appeared to be founded in jest, have become popular, such as the Church of Jediism. The line between a group that is created as a parody and one that seriously believes its own tenets is a fine one and occasionally a naïve believer may cross over from the former to the latter. For example, when I first heard of "Duane the Great Writer" – a surfer from Huntington Beach – and his many books touting the existence of Rebazar Tarzs, I thought it was done in jest, only to find out later that his teachings have garnered a number of very sincere followers.

Michael Turner is a good case in point. As far back as 1993, he began carving out his own path. Andrea Diem-Lane documents the events:

> Michael Turner, who had been a chela of Eckankar since the mid-1970s, eventually aligned himself with Darwin Gross' work, even serving as a facilitator for him and his ministry. However, in 1993 Turner started his own movement which he entitled The Sonic Spectrum. As Turner explains: "Since 1984, Sri Darwin Gross has taught a small coterie of chelas (probably less than 10,000 worldwide) [*sic*; the number is actually

much lower, closer to several hundred] as their Living Shabd Sat Guru. While I was indeed a chela of Sri Darwin's for many years, we severed all legal and contractual connections when I attained God realization and began teaching in late October 1993. This severance was a mutually agreed-upon decision which I initiated prior to my acceptance of mastership." (Diem-Lane 2015: 80–81)

Michael Turner offers instruction into shabd yoga, though without any of the restrictions other groups have demanded. He occasionally gives satsang on the Internet and in person, though the number of attendees is usually fewer than ten. Turner and others like him represent a new breed of gurus where one becomes established simply by creating a website or having a YouTube presence. One wonders what will be next with the increasing adoption of virtual and augmented technologies (Lane 2016a).

The Sound Current Tradition in Other Religions

1. Yogi Bhajan and 3HO

One of the most visible new religious movements in North America to emerge out of the 1960s was the Healthy, Happy, and Holy Organization (3HO) founded by Harbhajan Singh Khalsa (1929–2004). Formerly an airport customs inspector in Delhi, India, Yogi Bhajan, as he later became known, first emigrated to Canada and then began conducting yoga classes throughout North America. He created his own self-styled combination of kundalini yoga and Sikh teachings, along with a variety of health practices (including vegetarianism). His followers adopted white turbans and outfits and became a noticeable presence in California and New Mexico. Yogi Bhajan and his wife, Bibi Inderjit Kaur, were followers of Baba Virsa Singh, a Sikh spiritual master, but during a visit to India in 1971 there was a falling out. Pamela Saharah Dyson (aka Premka) indicates in her controversial book *Premka: White Bird in a Golden Cage* (2019) that the split between Baba Virsa Singh and Yogi Bhajan was over two issues – money and authority. Bhajan apparently didn't want to have his students aligned exclusively with Baba Virsa Singh and was upset that the money he had brought with him for proper accommodations was not forthcoming. The Sikh influence in Yogi Bhajan's group became much more apparent after this trip to India, where many received the Amrit ceremony of initiation in Sikhism and where they took on new names indicating their conversion. Yogi Bhajan's teachings incorporated the outward and inward chanting of mantras and listening to the inner sound current, much of it gleaned from his readings of Sikh scriptures in the Sri Guru Granth Sahib.

If you have mastered your mantra, the final stage of that will be whether you are sitting, walking, or talking, you are hearing it. All the time you hear your own mantra in the atmosphere.

If you master the sound current, you master the sound – that is, you master God.

This is the gift, this is sound current. It's a permutation and combination of sounds, which create waves to reach Infinity, and the Infinite brings infinite knowledge. (3HO.org 2022a)

The 3HO has centers throughout the world and offers a variety of classes, including a teaching specifically called "Shabad Guru," which Yogi Bhajan developed on the basis of his interpretation of Sikh scriptures. He explains:

The concept of the Shabad Guru is made in a very particular way. It is made in a very scientific way and it is very arty. Every shabad has a sound and that sound directs the intellect. The process to change a man out of his graveyard and to bring him to light is to rotate the stem of the brain which controls the vibratory continuous process of the intellect. The intellect gives you a thought on which intelligence is developed. The wisdom contains it and your human effort fulfills it. That is how the process works. What happens when you read Gurubani and pronounce it right is that you can change your whole everything – if you want to change.

(3HO.org 2022a)

In 1974 Yogi Bhajan and Kirpal Singh, the founder of Ruhani Satsang, became closely aligned at the Unity of Man Conference held in Delhi, India. There was even talk that Bhajan could be a successor to Kirpal Singh, despite the fact that he had never taken formal initiation. Bhajan recollects:

And I left all the way to India, and I asked [Kirpal] one thing which I loved in him. He said, "Well, I am going to die next year. You take over," and I said, "Forget it. That's not my job. I'm not going to take over anything from anybody. I have to do what I have to do." Then he said, "Well, this is the idea. Would you try to be second with me in this time?" I said, "All right, I'll do that." And in the end I almost was convinced that he is a great man. And he asked me, he said, "You don't believe in anybody except God, I mean to say. Human forms are very . . . I understand you, I know you," because he knows me from very childhood. But I asked him one thing. I said, "I have never seen a saint on whom saints believe. They all have their own territories and whole thing."

(Prabhupadabooks.com/ 1975)

After Yogi Bhajan died the 3HO weathered a major scandal when the Siri Singh Sahib Corporation commissioned an investigation into allegations of sexual and emotional abuse at the hands of Yogi Bhajan. The findings were released on August 13, 2020, and "concluded that much of the alleged conduct more likely than not occurred." The letter further stated in more detail that "SSSC and its related organizations are taking immediate action to address the findings of the report, assist reporters of harm, and promote healing in our community" (3HO.org 2022b).

It is not clear at this stage how 3HO will be impacted in the long term, though early indications are that, because the organization has acknowledged its leader's transgressions and has tried to make amends, it may distinguish its many programs from the founder's questionable lifestyle.

2. Ching Hai, Quan Yin, and God's Direct Contact Organization

One of the most popular shabd yoga-related movements in the world today is Ching Hai's God's Direct Contact (GDC), which teaches a meditation method known as Quan Yin, where the initiate focuses on the inner light and sound. Hue Dang Trinh (b. 1950), now honorifically called Ching Hai, was born in Vietnam and later established her ministry in Taiwan. Because of her strong advocacy of veganism, Ching Hai was the founder of Loving Hut restaurants, which have more than two hundred locations in thirty-five countries. It is the most visible outreach of her ministry, and besides offering plant-based food and drink, it serves as an informal introduction to Ching Hai's teachings.

Ching Hai was initiated into the sound current practice by Thakar Singh, who claimed to be Kirpal Singh's successor. Because of this association, one she has continually denied or downplayed, Ching Hai adopted several of Thakar's ideas, including keeping a daily spiritual diary and foregoing all animal products. In addition, Ching Hai mimics Thakar and Kirpal's key selling point that one will have a spiritual experience at the time of initiation. Although her meditation method is similar to that of Radhasoami, Ching Hai describes her sitting practice as Quan Yin, which is a spelling variation of Kuan-shi Yin, "the one that perceives the sounds of the world." The GDC's official website clearly explains the initiatory process:

> The initiation into the Quan Yin Method is not an esoteric ritual or a ceremony for entering a new religion. During the initiation, specific instruction in meditation on the inner Light and inner Sound is given, and Master Ching Hai provides the "Spiritual Transmission." This first taste of Divine Presence is given in silence. Master Ching Hai need not be physically present in order to open this "door" for you. The Transmission is an essential part of the Method. The techniques themselves will bring little benefit without the Grace of the Master. Because you may hear the inner Sound and see the inner Light immediately upon initiation, this event is sometimes referred to as "sudden" or "immediate" enlightenment. (Hai 2022)

Ching Hai asks her disciples to follow five precepts that are almost exactly the same requirements that all Radhasoami-related movements ask of their members. The one exception is precept five, where Radhasoami makes no stipulations about refraining from "gambling, pornography, and excessively violent films or literature."

1. Refrain from taking the life of sentient beings. This precept requires strict adherence to a vegan diet. No meat, fish, poultry or eggs (fertilized or nonfertilized).
2. Refrain from speaking what is not true.
3. Refrain from taking what is not yours.
4. Refrain from sexual misconduct.
5. Refrain from using intoxicants. This includes avoiding all poisons of any kind, such as alcohol, drugs, tobacco, gambling, pornography, and excessively violent films or literature (Hai 2022).

Although Ching Hai's teachings have often been compared to certain Mahayana schools of Buddhism, the fact remains that they share much more in common with Sant Mat and Radhasoami. Indeed the spiritual diary she advised her followers to use was a verbatim copy of the one that Kirpal Singh and several of his successors, including Thakar Singh, Ching Hai's one-time guru, advised their initiates to use (Ruhanisatsangusa.org 2022).

Ching Hai represents a new wave in those teaching sound current meditation, since she is the first female shabd yoga guru to have a worldwide following. Although the vast majority of her followers are Asian, she has attracted seekers from almost all nationalities and ethnic heritages. Ching Hai has also made shabd yoga accessible to a new audience because of her ability to connect with Chinese and Vietnamese diasporic communities. By connecting to her Buddhist background and calling her meditational technique Quan Yin, rather than the Indian terms *shabd* or *nad yoga*, Ching Hai has legitimized listening to the inner sound current as a practice that dovetails with the teachings of Buddha and his millions of followers. The original definition of Quan Yin, usually spelled Guan Yin or Kuan Yin in Chinese, refers to the compassionate Buddha. Ching Hai may have adopted the phrase, with her stylized spelling, since it is the shortened version of Guanshiyin, which, according to the Nichiren school of Buddhism, means "perceiver of the world's sounds" (Soka Gakkai n.d.). However, in its original context this Bodhisattva is one who responds to the suffering pleas of living beings across the globe. It is not at all clear that the term is a subtle reference to listening to the sound current during meditation.

3. The Sound Current in Jainism and Buddhism

While listening to the sound current is prevalent in Sufism, Nathism, Santism, Radhasoami, and various related movements, select schools of Jainism and Buddhism also incorporate nad/shabd yoga into their meditational disciplines. For example, Acharya Sushil Kumar (1926–1994), a well-known Jain leader who established the first Jain Tirtha or pilgrimage center, Siddhāchalam, in North America, advocated the practice of Arhum Yoga. Pravin K. Shah elaborates.

> Guruji was a self realized master, well known for his practice of effects of sound on spiritual progress and his teachings of the Arhum Yoga system. Arhum Yoga is an ancient system for the mastery of the inner self through watchfulness and direct perception. It encompasses all aspects of philosophy and yogic practice in the Arihant tradition. It includes the Eight Steps of Yoga, sound vibration, healing, awakening of the kundalini and all divine powers, color science, holistic health, the concepts of Ahimsa, Anekantvad, and the perfection of the soul. This knowledge is based on the Matrika Vidya of the Namokar Mantra which is the foremost mantra in the Jain tradition holding much secret knowledge. (Shah 2022)

Acharya Sushil Kumar's understanding of Arhum yoga may have been influenced, at least in part, by his close association with Kirpal Singh, Darshan Singh, and other shabd yoga mystics, including Baba Faqir Chand, who were also strong advocates of listening to the inner sound current. During our personal interview with Acharya Sushil Kumar in 1983 at his temporary residence in Long Beach, California, he remarked that listening to the sound current had a long tradition in India and was known among Jain leaders and monks, though not widely publicized. He was intensely interested in making Jain doctrines and spiritual aspirations much more accessible to an educated populace that had turned away from religion and had adopted a more scientific approach to life. The Jain leader wanted to seek the unity of all religions and, in that spirit, he saw that the essence of ahimsa (nonviolence) and anekantavada (holding multiple viewpoints) were universal ethical ideals.

Kumar further explained that the key to ending war was to transcend the self and the feeling of others being different. "Instead [he] argues for finding the source from which all violent tendencies spring forth." If that area becomes our focus, he contended, then the question of a third world war would not even arise – much less the weapons in preparation for it. But what is it that drives us toward aggression? Is it biologically preprogrammed? Does environment, via our social structures, breed it? We had planned to pose these very questions to Sushil Kumar, but within five minutes from our initial meeting he had already answered them in a brilliant fashion. His response, which is echoed in the ancient Upanishads, is perhaps simpler than one might expect: "Wherever there is another, fear arises. It is the emergence of the separate self – the 'I-ness,' the egoic structure – which is at the heart of man's cruelty." With the advent of self-awareness also comes the presumption of what is "not self," and all of that (the environment, the world, "them") generates fear. This fear drives human beings to protect the self from all that threatens its separate existence. But such a strategy can only end in failure and a lifelong narcissism, a denial of the universe and what it offers. Paradoxically, the more one tries to retain the self, the more one eventually loses it in the fight against the "not self" (the world). A tragic double bind indeed! What is the solution? There's only one, Sushil Kumar postulates. "Give up the false idea of an independent self and begin to see the creation as one indivisible whole" (Lane 2014: 37–43).

There are also aspects of nad yoga in Buddhism, although not nearly as explicit as in Sant Mat and Sikhism. Several Buddhist writings provide instructions that the aspirant should find the source from which the sound arises, which ultimately is in the no-sound or stillness. Ajahn Sumedho, author of *The Way It Is* (1991), and former abbot of the Amaravati Buddhist Monastery in the United Kingdom, argues that "the sound of silence" is an elemental meditation practice. Some Buddhist monks and scholars argue that the Śūraṅgama Sūtra in Buddhism contains nad yoga teachings, though how to properly interpret this text is still open to varying interpretations.

> Ananda, if a man suddenly closes his ears with two fingers, disturbance will arise in this sense organ and he will hear sounds in his head.
>
> (Buddhanet 2022: 92)

Ajahn Sumedho and Ajahn Amaro admit they were influenced in their understanding of sound current yoga by Edward Salim Michael (1921–2006), a distinguished musical composer who is the author of *The Law of Attention: Nada Yoga and the Way of Inner Vigilance* (2010). Amaro connects the practice to earlier Buddhist meditations:

> As you calm down, you can experience the sound of silence in the mind. You hear it as a kind of high frequency sound, a ringing sound that's always there. It is just normally never noticed. Now when you begin to hear that sound of silence, it's a sign of emptiness – of silence of the mind. It's something you can always turn to. As you concentrate on it and turn to it, it can make you quite peaceful and blissful. Meditating on that, you have a way of letting the conditions of the mind cease without suppressing them with another condition.
>
> (Amaro 2012: 72)

Because of the efforts of the Amaravati monastery and publication department, the practice of nada yoga has become more widely discussed in Buddhist circles and there is a continued effort to find how listening to the inner sound current is resonant with Buddha and Buddhism in the quest to achieve nirvana.

Conclusion

Today listening to the inner sound current is a well-established practice across a number of religious movements, old and new. The technical aspects of shabd yoga are no longer an esoteric secret known only to the privileged few. Shabd and nad yoga have a long tradition as we have seen, dating back to the Vedic period in India, and they are now a transcultural phenomenon not restricted to any single country or ethnicity. However, a number of questions remain concerning how to best interpret the inner sound current, with believers and skeptics positing different theories. These range from the purely reductionistic (noises in the head are symptoms of tinnitus) to the transcendent (divine music that leads to enlightenment). What should not be overlooked here is that there is a spectrum of possibilities concerning the various sounds one hears during meditation, since even acknowledged masters of the tradition, such as Sawan Singh of Radha Soami Satsang Beas, readily admit that some sounds are merely local or due to purely physiological causes. Even if shabd or nad is explained via the brain and the nervous system, it does not therefore mean it is a singular sensation, since there are grosser and subtler variations in what one hears. Some sounds are musical and uplifting and generate tremendous bliss, whereas others cause anxiety and even headaches. Simply put, a truly scientific understanding of shabd/nad yoga is still in its infancy.

What is perhaps most intriguing is to see how consistent the technical aspects of listening to the inner sound current have been since time immemorial. Essentially, it is the closing of one's ears so the aspirant can better hear what has hitherto mostly gone by unnoticed. The process for doing this is usually twofold. First is assuming a squatting position, such as the malasana posture, and using the knees as leverages to rest one's elbow, freeing the thumbs to plug both ears; second is using a T-stick – in SRF it is known as an AUM board – and resting the elbows on each side to make it easier to plug both ears with one's hands. There are other methods, such as simply sitting quietly and not using the hands to ward off outer noises, but these are usually employed after one has become adept at hearing the inner sound current during most hours of the day.

It is perhaps a bit surprising to learn that these simple techniques have been cloaked in secrecy among a number of spiritual movements for centuries, as if knowing how to correctly listen to the shabd is a taboo subject and should only be taught to those who are deserving of initiation. Indeed one of the attractive advantages of many sound current movements such as Radhasoami and Eckankar is that becoming a member of the organization will allow the neophyte to have access to arcane knowledge that they could not receive otherwise. One of Kirpal Singh's most alluring advertisements was that he could actually confer experiences of light and sound during meditation to his students, suggesting that a master of the tradition has the ability to directly transmit glimpses of the transcendent. But after his death – with so many successors claiming to have the same spiritual power – it became obvious that it was the meditator herself, and not the initiating guru, who was generating the inner fireworks. The esteemed shabd yoga master Baba Faqir Chand (1886–1981) was adamant that gurus and masters have no such power and that their respective students wrongly impute powers to them that they do not have. In his view it was the faith and belief of the disciple, not the teacher, that produced the stupendous results. As Faqir confessed, "Now, you see no Jesus Christ comes from without in anybody's visions. No Rama, no Krishna, no Buddha, and no Baba Faqir come from without to anybody. The visions are only because of the impressions and suggestions that a disciple has already accepted in his mind. These impressions and suggestions appear to him like a dream. No body comes from without. This is the plain truth" (Lane 2018a: 21). From a neurological perspective, one can reframe Faqir's argument and suggest that it is the brain's own capacity to engender magnificent experiences of light and sound and that gurus merely tapped into that pre-existing mechanism.

Clearly, the early Indian writings on the subject – from the Nadabindu Upanishad to the *Hatha Yoga Pradipika* to the *Gheranda Samhita* – have had a significant influence on later yoga movements, particularly in articulating what sounds one should attend to during meditation. In modern times the most influential books on the subject have been Madame Blavatsky's original 1889 *Voice of the Silence* (2015), Julian P. Johnson's *With a Great Master in India* (1934) and *The Path of the Masters* (1939), Kirpal Singh's *Crown of Life* (1973) and *Naam or Word* (1974), Paul Twitchell's *The Tiger's Fang* (1967), and, most recently, Edward Salim Michael's *The Law of Attention: Nada Yoga and the Way of Inner Vigilance* (2010).

It seems certain that shabd yoga meditation and its various iterations will continue to become more popular in the future, depending in part on the success of new religious movements such as Ching Hai's Quan Yin teachings, Radhasoami and its various branches, and the emergence of nonsectarian groups that promote listening to the inner sound without requiring initiation or following a guru.

Technology can also play a key role with the advent of new meditational aids such as brain-sensing headbands that provide the meditator with instant feedback. In addition, virtual and augmented reality headsets are primed to offer new pathways for deeper sound current meditations, since they can provide environments conducive for one via digital instruction, guided by preset and adaptable artificially intelligent algorithms.

With mindfulness meditation and other forms of relaxation becoming increasingly popular around the world, we should expect that shabd yoga-related movements will continue to flourish, though perhaps in ways we cannot yet predict.

Bibliography

Books and Articles

3HO.org (2022a). "3HO Letter on Investigation Findings." https://www.3ho .org/blog-new/august-2020-community-update/

3HO.org (2022b). "What Is Shabad Guru?" www.3ho.org/articles/what-shabd-guru. Offline May 16, 2022.

Acoustical Society of America. (2017). "Want to Listen Better? Lend a Right Ear." *Science Daily*. October. https://www.sciencedaily.com/releases/2017/ 12/171206090611.htm

Aiyar, N. K., trans. (1914). *Thirty Minor Upanishads*. Madras, India: Madras.

Albrecht, M., & Alexander, B. (1979). "Eckankar, a Hard Look at a New Religion: Special Issue." *SCP Journal* 3(1).

Amaro, A. (2012). "Buddhism and the Sound Current: Transcendental Hearing." https://www.speakingtree.in/blog/buddhism-and-the-sound-cur rent-transcendental-hearing

Anandpur Trust (1975). *Sri Paramhans Advait Mat*. Ashoknagar, India: Shri Anandpur Trust.

Asiri, F. M., ed. and trans. (2021). *The Mystic Sublime: Rubaiyat-I-Sarmad*. Walnut, CA: Mt. San Antonio College.

Barthwal, P. D. (1978). *Traditions of Indian Mysticism Based upon Nirguna School of Hindi Poetry*. Delhi: Heritage Press.

Bean, J. (2017). "Maharaj Girdhari Sahib: The Unknown Guru of Radhasoami History." *Sach Khand: Journal of Radhasoami Studies*, Special Issue.

Beck, G. L. (2009). *Sonic Theology: Hinduism and Sacred Sound*. Columbia: University of South Carolina Press.

Bellamy, D. (1995). "Former Eckankar Re-visits the Movement: Hi Fubbi, This Is Gakko." *San Diego Reader*. www.sandiegoreader.com/news/1995/jun/22/ cover-fraud-eckankar

Berger, P. (1979). *The Heretical Imperative: Contemporary Possibilities of Religious Affirmation*. Norwell, MA: Anchor/Doubleday.

Bhagatsinghthind.com (2022). www.bhagatsinghthind.com/about/na%CC% 83m-the-sound-within

Blackmore, S. (2000). *The Meme Machine*. Oxford: Oxford University Press.

Blavatsky, H. P. (2015). *The Voice of the Silence*. Pasadena, CA: Theosophical University Press.

Böhme, J. (1914). *Aurora*. London: John M. Watkins.

Brooks, P. L., & Peever, J. H. (2012). "Identification of the Transmitter and Receptor Mechanisms Responsible for REM Sleep Paralysis." *Journal of Neuroscience* 32(29), 9785–95.

Brunton, P. (1985). *A Search in Secret India*. New York: Samuel Weiser.

Buddhanet (2022). www.buddhanet.net/pdf_file/surangama.pdf

Caesar, E. (2020). *The Moth and the Mountain: A True Story of Love, War, and Everest*. New York: Simon & Schuster.

Caldwell, D. (2004). "Notes on Rai Salig Ram, Shiva Dayal Singh, etc." *Theos-Talk Archives* (November 30). https://www.blavatskyarchives.com/Caldwell_Who_Is_Suby_Ram.pdf

Chandra, A. (2019). *Dara Shukoh: The Man Who Would Be King*. New Delhi: HarperCollins.

Churchland, P. (1986). *Neurophilosophy: Toward a Unified Science of the Mind-Brain*. Cambridge, MA: MIT Press.

Cranston, S. (1993). *H.P.B.: The Extraordinary Life & Influence of Helena Blavatsky Founder of the Modern Theosophical Movement*. Los Angeles: TarcherPerigee.

Davisson. D. M. (2020). *Wipe: A Brief History of Toilet Hygiene*. N.p. Hillsborough River Press.

Dawkins, R. (1976). *The Selfish Gene*. Oxford: Oxford University Press.

Dayalbagh Educational Institute (2021). https://www.dei.ac.in/dei/DSC2021/?page_id=1033

De La Garza, A. (2010). *Doctorji: The Life, Teachings, and Legacy of Dr. Bhagat Singh Thind*. Malibu, CA: David Bhagat Thind.

Dhyansky, Y. Y. (1987). "The Indus Valley Origin of a Yoga Practice." *Artibus Asiae*, 48(1/2), 89–108.

Diem, A. (1992). *The Gnostic Mystery: A Connection between Ancient and Modern Mysticism*. Walnut, CA: Mt. San Antonio College.

Diem-Lane, A. (2015). *The Guru in America*. Walnut, CA: Mt. San Antonio College.

Diem-Lane, A., & Lane, D. C. (2018). *Listening to the Inner Sound Current: The Perennial Practice of Shabd Yoga*. Walnut, CA: Mt. San Antonio College.

Diem-Lane, A., & Lane, D. C. (2020). *The Master Plagiarist: Gary Olsen and MasterPath*. Walnut: Mt. San Antonio College.

Doran, M. (2019). *The Neural Basis of Consciousness: An Interview with Professor Patricia Churchland*. Walnut, CA: Mt. San Antonio College.

Dudeja, J. (2018). "Analysis and Benefits of Chant-less Sohum/Humsa Mantra Meditation." *Sports Engineering* 3(2), 198–203.

Dyczkowski, M. S. G. (1987). *The Doctrine of Vibration: An Analysis of the Doctrines and Practices of Kashmir Shaivism.* Albany: State University of New York Press.

Dyson, P. S. (2019). *Premka: White Bird in a Golden Cage: My Life with Yogi Bhajan.* Maui, HI: Eyes Wide.

Eckankar.org (2022).

Eliade, M. (1970). *Yoga: Immortality and Freedom.* Princeton, NJ: Princeton University Press.

Ernst, C., & Lawrence, B. (2002). *Sufi Martyrs of Love: The Chishti Order in South Asia and Beyond.* London: Palgrave Macmillan.

Field, C. (2020). *Mullah Shah: The Sufi Mystic.* Walnut, CA: Mt. San Antonio College.

Forman, M., & Fishelman, L. (2014). "Swami Muktananda & Stroke: The Untold Medical Story of a Brilliant Guru's Tarnished Legacy." *Elephant Journal* (September 15). www.elephantjournal.com/2014/09/swami-muktananda-and-stroke-the-untold-medical-story-of-a-brilliant-gurus-tarnished-legacy

Garrett, E. (1895). *Isis Very Much Unveiled.* London: Westminster Gazette Office.

Giri, S. S. (2021). *Yogananda Sanga: As I Have Seen and Understood Him.* Kolkata, India: Prajna.

Godsdirectcontact.org.

Goodman, F. D. (2008). *Speaking in Tongues: A Cross-Cultural Study of Glossolalia.* Eugene, OR: Wipf and Stock.

Gorakhbodh (2007). https://dharmabindu.com/?l=pt&p=ensinamento&id=135

Hai, C. (2022). "The Quan Yin Method." *God's Direct Contact.* www .godsdirectcontact.org/eng/quanyin.html

Hare, E., & Hare, W. L. (1936). *Who Wrote the Mahatma Letters? The First Thorough Examination of the Communications Alleged to Have Been Received by the Late A.P. Sinnett from Tibetan Mahatmas.* London: Williams & Norgate.

Hariharananda, P. (1992). *The Original and Authentic Kriya Yoga of Babaji Maharaj and Lahiri Mahasaya.* Canoga Park, CA: Kriya Yoga Ashram.

Harris, L. (1994). "O Guru, Guru, Guru." *New Yorker* (November 7). www .newyorker.com/magazine/1994/11/14

Harris, S. (2014). *Waking Up: A Guide to Spirituality without Religion.* New York: Simon & Schuster.

History Matters. (2022). "Not All Caucasians Are White: The Supreme Court Rejects Citizenship for Asian Americans." 1923. http://historymatters.gmu .edu/d/5076.

Holtje, D. (1995). *From Light to Sound: The Spiritual Progression.* Temecula, CA: Blue Star.

Johnson, F. (2003). *Confessions of a God Seeker: A Journey to Higher Consciousness.* Silver Spring, MD: "One" Publishing.

Johnson, J. P. (1939). *The Path of the Masters.* Beas, India: Sawan Service League.

Johnson, J. P. (1934, 1953). *With a Great Master in India.* Beas, India: Sawan Service League.

Johnson, K. P. (1994). *The Masters Revealed: Madame Blavatsky and the Myth of the Great White Lodge.* Albany: State University of New York Press.

Johnson, K. P. (1998). *Edgar Cayce in Context: The Readings: Truth and Fiction.* Albany: State University of New York Press.

Juergensmeyer, M. (1991). *Radhasoami Reality: The Logic of a Modern Faith.* Princeton, NJ: Princeton University Press.

Kapur, D. L. (1994). *Heaven on Earth.* Beas, India: Radha Soami Satsang.

Kaushal O. P. (1998). *The Radha Soami Movement.* Jalandhar, India: ABS.

Khan, H. I. (1996). *The Mysticism of Sound and Music.* Boulder, CO: Shambhala.

Khan, H. I. (2019). *The Mystic Sound.* Walnut, CA: Mt. San Antonio College.

Krishnananda, S. (1997). *The Māndūkya Upanishad.* Rishikesh, India: Sivananda Ashram, E-book. www.swami-krishnananda.org/mand/Mandukya_Upanishad.pdf

Kriyananda, S. (1988). *The Path: Autobiography of a Western Yogi.* Commerce, CA: Crystal Clarity.

Kugle, S. and Ernst, C., eds. and trans. (2012). *Sufi Meditation and Contemplation: Timeless Wisdom from Mughal India.* New York: Omega.

Lane, D. C. (1983). *The Making of a Spiritual Movement: The Untold Story of Paul Twitchell and Eckankar.* Del Mar, CA: Del Mar Press.

Lane, D. C. (1984). "The J.R. Controversy: A Critical Analysis of John-Roger Hinkins and M.S.I.A." *Understanding Cults and Spiritual Movements* 1(1).

Lane, D. C. (1992). *The Radhasoami Tradition.* New York & London: Garland.

Lane, D. C. (2014). *The Enchanted Land.* Walnut: CA: Mt. San Antonio College.

Lane, D. C. (2016a). *The Avatar Project: Virtual Reality, A.I., and the Future of Education.* Walnut: Mt. San Antonio College.

Lane, D. C., ed. (2016b). *The Gnostic Jesus: Esoteric Christianity.* Walnut, CA: Mt. San Antonio College.

Lane, D. C. (2017a). *The Mystery of Dr. Johnson's Death: A Spiritual Scandal in the Punjab.* Walnut, CA: Mt. San Antonio College.

Lane, D. C. (2017b). *The Succession Conspiracy*. Walnut, CA: Mt. San Antonio College.

Lane, D. C. (2018a). *Inner Visions and Running Trains*. Walnut, CA: Mt. San Antonio College.

Lane, D. C. (2018b). *Rai Salig Ram: A Glimpse of His Life and Work*. Walnut, CA: Mt. San Antonio College.

Lane, D. C. (2019a). *A Beacon of Light*. Walnut, CA: Mt. San Antonio College.

Lane, D. C. (2019b). *The Virtual Reality of Consciousness*. Walnut, CA: Mt. San Antonio College.

Lane, D.C., ed. (2019c). *Kabir: Selected Poems from Sri Guru Granth Sahib*. Walnut, CA: Mt. San Antonio College.

Lane, D. C. (2020a). *Gakko Came from Venus: Exploring the Lost History of Eckankar*. Walnut, CA: Mt. San Antonio College.

Lane, D. C. (2020b). *The Skeptical Yogi*. Walnut, CA: Mt. San Antonio College.

Lane, D. C., & Diem-Lane, A. (2018). *Listening to the Inner Sound*. Walnut, CA: Mt. San Antonio College.

Lane, D. C., & Diem-Lane, A. (2020). *The Master Plagiarist*. Walnut, CA: Mt. San Antonio College.

Lewis, J. R. (1998). *Seeking the Light: Uncovering the Truth about the Movement of Spiritual Inner Awareness and Its Founder John-Roger*. Los Angeles: Mandeville Press.

Lokeswarananda, S. (2017). *Chandogya Upanisad: Following Sankara's Commentary*. With Sanskrit Text, Transliteration, Translation and Notes. Hyderabad, India: Ramakrishna Math.

Mallinson, J., trans. (2004). *The Gheranda Samhita*. Woodstock, NY: YogaVidya.com.

Mann, J. (2014). *Before the Sun: Meeting Rudi*. Seattle, WA: CreateSpace Independent.

Marman, D. (2007). *The Whole Truth: The Spiritual Legacy of Paul Twitchell*. Spiritual Dialogues Project. https://spiritualdialogues.com

Mayo Clinic. (2022). *Tinnitus: Overview*. https://www.mayoclinic.org/dis eases-conditions/tinnitus/symptoms-causes/syc-20350156

McLeod, W. H., & Schomer, K. (1987). *The Sants Studies in a Devotional Tradition of India*. Delhi: Motilal Banarsidass.

McWilliams, P. (1994). *Life 102: What to Do When Your Guru Sues You*. Los Angeles: Prelude Press.

Meade, M. (2014). *Madame Blavatsky, the Woman behind the Myth*. New York: Open Road Media.

Michael, E. S. (2010). *The Law of Attention: Nada Yoga and the Way of Inner Vigilance*. 2nd ed. Rochester, VT: Inner Traditions.

MSIA.org. (2022). www.msia.org/faqs

Muktananda, S. (1971). *The Play of Consciousness*. New York: Siddha Yoga Dham.

Soka Gakkai (n.d.) "Perceiver of the World's Sounds." *Nicheren Buddhism Library*. www.nichirenlibrary.org/en/dic/Content/P/39.

Nivedita, B. (1910). *The Master As I Saw Him*. London: Longmans, Green, and Company.

Olsen, G. (1999). *MasterPath: The Divine Science of Light and Sound*. Temecula, CA: MasterPath.

Olsen, G. (2005). *Soul's Divine Journey*. Temecula, CA: MasterPath.

Paul, R. (2006). *The Yoga of Sound: The Healing Power of Chant and Mantra*. Novato, CA: New World Library.

Prabhupadabooks.com/. (1975) https://prabhupadabooks.com/conversations/1975/jun/with_yogi_bhajan/honolulu/june/07/1975

Prakashananda, S. (2007). *Baba Muktananda: A Biography*. Mountain View, CA: Sarasvati Productions.

Prem Rawat Biography. (2022). http://prem-rawat-bio.org/begone.html

Prem Rawat official http://prem-rawat-bio.org/satsang/shrihans_satsang.html

Puri, I. (2022). https://ishanews.org/letters-to-ishwar

Robinson, J. (1979). *Truth Is Two-Eyed*. Philadelphia, PA: Westminster Press.

Roger-Hinkins, J. (1976. *The Sound Current*. Los Angeles: MSIA.

Rogo, D. S. (1970). *NAD: A Study of Some Unusual "Other-World" Experiences*. New York: University Books.

Rogo, D. S. (1972). *A Psychic Study of "the Music of the Spheres."* NAD, vol. 2. Seacaucus, NJ: University Books.

Rolle, R. (1996). *The Fire of Love and the Mending of Life or the Rule of Living*. Woodbridge, UK: Boydell & Brewer.

Ruhanisatsangusa.org. (2022). www.ruhanisatsangusa.org

Samuels, D. (2020). *The Seeker and the Sought*. Meadville, PA: Christian Faith Publishing.

Shah, P. K. (2022). *Jain Quantum*. https://jainqq.org/explore/200011/1

Shaktipat Intensive. (n.d.) "The Siddha Yoga Shaktipat Intensive." www.siddhayoga.org/shaktipat-intensive

Sharpless, B. A., & Barber, J. P. (2011). "Lifetime Prevalence Rates of Sleep Paralysis: A Systematic Review." *Sleep Medical Review* 155, 311–315.

Shikoh, D. (2020). *Compass of Truth: The Esoteric Practice of Sultan-ul-Azkar*. Rai Bahadur Srisa Chandra Vasu, trans. Walnut, CA: Mt. San Antonio College.

Siddhayoga.org (2022a). www.siddhayoga.org/baba-muktananda-mahasamadhi/ teachings-from-baba/nada

Siddhayoga.org (2022b).

Singh, C. (1999). *Die to Live*. Beas, India: Radha Soami Satsang.

Singh, J. (1959). *The Science of the Soul*. Beas, India: Radha Soami Satsang.

Singh, K. (1960). *A Great Saint, Baba Jaimal Singh, His Life and Teaching*. Delhi: Ruhani Satsang.

Singh, K. (1967). *Spiritual Elixir, Book Two*. Delhi: Ruhani Satsang.

Singh, K. (1973). *Crown of Life*. Delhi: Ruhani Satsang.

Singh, K. (1976). *Heart to Heart Talks*, vol. 1. Malcolm Tillis, ed. Delhi: Ruhani Satsang.

Singh, K. (2017). *Naam or Word*. Blaine, WA: Ruhani Satsang.

Singh, P. (1978). *Biography of Soamiji Maharaj*. S. D. Maheshwari, trans. Agra, India: Soami Bagh.

Singh, S. B. J. (1959). *The Science of the Soul*. Beas, India: Radha Soami Satsang Beas.

Singh, S. (1963). *Discourses on Sant Mat*. Beas, India: Radha Soami Satsang.

Singh, S. *Spiritual Gems*. (1965). Beas, India: Radha Soami Satsang.

Sinh, P., trans. (1914). *Hatha Yoga Pradipika*. Allahabad, India: Panini Office.

Sinnett, A. P. (1923). *The Mahatma Letters*. London: T. F. Unwin.

Spencer, C. (2011). *Pathways to Peace: Understanding "Death" and Embracing Life*. Bloomington, IN: Balboa Press.

Sriamamurti, P., Prashant, P. & Mohan, A., eds. (2013). *Spiritual Consciousness*. New Delhi: New Age Books.

Sumedho, A. (1991). *The Way It Is*. Hemel Hempstead, UK: Amaravati.

Tagore, R. (2016). *Kabir: A Poetic Glimpse of His Life and Work*. Walnut, CA: Mt. San Antonio College.

Tessler, N. (2017). *Crisis and Renewal*. Seattle, WA: CreateSpace Independent.

Theosociety. (2022). www.theosociety.org/pasadena/ts/silence.htm

Thind, B. S. (1939). *Radiant Road to Reality*. New York: privately published.

Twitchell, P. (1967). *The Tiger's Fang*. Menlo Park, CA: Illuminated Way Press.

Twitchell, P. (1971a). *The Far Country*. Menlo Park, CA: Illuminated Way Press.

Twitchell, P. (1971b). *Shariyat-ki-Sugmad*. Menlo Park, CA: Illuminated Way Press.

Twitchell, P. (1971c). *The Spiritual Notebook*. Menlo Park, CA: Illuminated Way Press.

Upadhyaya, K. N. (2010). *Buddhism: Path to Nirvana*. Beas, India: Radha Soami Satsang Beas.

Vasu, S. C. (1979). *Gheranda Samhita*. Delhi: Indian Book Centre.

Yogananda, P. (1946). *Autobiography of a Yogi*. New York: Philosophical Library.

Yogananda.org (2022). http://yogananda.com.au/sc/sc06om.html

Yukteswar, S. S. (2020). *The Holy Science*. Quicktime Press.

Zoccatelli, P. (2006). "Ancient Teachings of the Masters." In P. Clarke, ed., *Encyclopedia of New Religious Movements*, 32–33. London: Routledge.

New Sound Current Movements Websites

Ajaib Singh. Sant Bani Ashram. https://santbaniashram.org/sant-ajaib-satsangs

Baba Faqir Chand. Manavta Mandir. http://manavtamandir.com

Baljit Singh. Know Thyself. www.knowthyselfassoul.org

Ching Hai/Quan Yin. www.godsdirectcontact.org

Christopher Tims. www.christophertims.com

Darwin Gross. Ancient Teachings of the Masters (ATOM). www.atom.org

Dr. Bhagat Singh Thind. www.bhagatsinghthind.com

Duane the Great Writer. www.duanethegreatwriter.net

Eckankar, Harold Klemp. www.eckankar.org

The Eureka Society. www.theeurekasociety.org

Ishwar Puri. ISHA. https://ishanews.org

Gurinder Singh. Radha Soami Satsang Beas. https://rssb.org

John-Roger Hinkins/John Morton: MSIA. www.msia.org

Kriya Yoga International. www.kriya.org

Michael Turner/Spiritual Freedom Satsang. https://spiritualfreedomsatsang.org/index.html

Prem Rawat. www.premrawat.com.

Rajinder Singh. Science of Spirituality. www.sos.org/sos-global

Ram Singh. http://santramsinghji.org

Sadhu Ram. www.mediaseva.com

Siddha Yoga International. www.siddhayoga.org

Sri Gary Olsen. MasterPath. www.masterpath.org

Swami Kriyananda. www.ananda.org

The Theosophical Society in America. www.theosophical.org/about/theosophy

Vardankar. http://vardankar.com

Yogi Bhajan. Healthy, Happy, Holy Organization (3HO). www.3ho.org

Films on the History and Practice of Shabd Yoga on YouTube

1. *Hanging on the Gallows: Baba Faqir Chand and the Tibetan Book of the Dead.* https://youtu.be/EGpCa6nZM3A
2. *Listening to the Inner Sound: The Perennial Practice of Shabd Yoga.* https://youtu.be/PkSCgbzFi7c

3. *Sawan Singh and the Way of Sound.* https://youtu.be/c8k4yXuGH28
4. *The Ancient Practice of Shabd Yoga.* https://youtu.be/zZIip8x6-BM
5. *The Future of Meditation: Technological Augmentation and Interior Sojourns.* https://youtu.be/EIAyFL5LF-s
6. *The Mystic Sound: Hazrat Inayat Khan.* https://youtu.be/u5wMi1kPhJo
7. *The Radhasoami Connection: Exploring the Influence of Shiv Dayal Singh.* https://youtu.be/Mdl5DNhaf-8
8. *The Sound Current: A Meditational Session on Shabd and Nam.* https://youtu.be/5AMHtl4q3t8

To my wife, Dr. Andrea Diem-Lane and to our two sons, Kelly and Shaun

Cambridge Elements ☰

New Religious Movements

Series Editors

James R. Lewis
Wuhan University

James R. Lewis is Professor of Philosophy at Wuhan University, China. He currently edits or co-edits four book series, is the general editor for the *Alternative Spirituality and Religion Review* and the associate editor for the *Journal of Religion and Violence*. His publications include *The Cambridge Companion to Religion and Terrorism* (Cambridge University Press 2017) and *Falun Gong: Spiritual Warfare and Martyrdom* (Cambridge University Press 2018).

Rebecca Moore
San Diego State University

Rebecca Moore is Emerita Professor of Religious Studies at San Diego State University. She has written numerous books and articles on Peoples Temple and the Jonestown tragedy. Publications include *Beyond Brainwashing: Perspectives on Cultic Violence* (Cambridge University Press 2018) and *Peoples Temple and Jonestown in the Twenty-First Century* (Cambridge University Press 2022). She is reviews editor for *Nova Religio*, the quarterly journal on new and emergent religions published by University of California Press.

About the Series

Elements in New Religious Movements go beyond cult stereotypes and popular prejudices to present new religions and their adherents in a scholarly and engaging manner. Case studies of individual groups, such as Transcendental Meditation and Scientology, provide in-depth consideration of some of the most well known, and controversial, groups. Thematic examinations of women, children, science, technology, and other topics focus on specific issues unique to these groups. Historical analyses locate new religions in specific religious, social, political, and cultural contexts. These examinations demonstrate why some groups exist in tension with the wider society and why others live peaceably in the mainstream. The series demonstrates the differences, as well as the similarities, within this great variety of religious expressions. To discuss contributing to this series please contact Professor Moore.

Cambridge Elements ≡

New Religious Movements

Elements in the Series

A full series listing is available at: www.cambridge.org/ENRM

Printed in the United States
by Baker & Taylor Publisher Services